Brad Miser

Sams **Teach Yourself**

iTunes® 10

in **10 Minutes**

SAMS | 800 East 96th Street, Indianapolis, Indiana 46240

Sams Teach Yourself iTunes 10 in 10 Minutes

ISBN-13: 978-0-672-334337
ISBN-10: 0-672-33433-X

Library of Congress Cataloging-in-Publication Data

Miser, Brad.
  iTunes in 10 minutes / Brad Miser.
    p. cm. — (Sams teach yourself)
  Includes index.
  ISBN 978-0-672-33433-7
  1. iTunes. 2. Digital jukebox software. I. Title.
  ML74.4.I49M62 2011
  006.5—dc22

                        2010046973

Printed in the United States of America

First Printing December 2010

Trademarks

Warning and Disclaimer

Bulk Sales

Pearson offers excellent discounts on this book when ordered in quantity for bulk purchases or special sales. For more information, please contact

    U.S. Corporate and Government Sales
    1-800-382-3419
    corpsales@pearsontechgroup.com

For sales outside of the U.S., please contact

    International Sales
    international@pearsoned.com

Associate Publisher
Greg Wiegand

Aquisitions Editor
Laura Norman

Development Editor
Keith Cline

Technical Editor
Jennifer Kettell

Managing Editor
Kristy Hart

Project Editor
Lori Lyons

Indexer
Cheryl Lenser

Proofreader
Apostrophe Editing Services

Publishing Coordinator
Cindy Teeters

Book Designer
Gary Adair

Compositor
Nonie Ratcliff

Contents

About the Author

Brad Miser has written extensively about technology, with his favorite topics being Apple's amazing "i" products, including iTunes, iPods, and iPhones. Books Brad has written include *My iPod touch, 2nd Edition*; *My iPhone, 4th Edition*; *Easy iLife '09*; *Special Edition Using Mac OS X Leopard*; *Absolute Beginner's Guide to Homeschooling*; *Teach Yourself Visually MacBook Air*; and *MacBook Pro Portable Genius, 2nd Edition*. He has also been an author, development editor, or technical editor on more than 50 other titles.

Brad is or has been a sales support specialist, the director of product and customer services, and the manager of education and support services for several software development companies. Previously, he was the lead proposal specialist for an aircraft engine manufacturer, a development editor for a computer book publisher, and a civilian aviation test officer/engineer for the U.S. Army. Brad holds a Bachelor of Science degree in mechanical engineering from California Polytechnic State University at San Luis Obispo and has received advanced education in maintainability engineering, business, and other topics.

Originally from California, Brad now lives in Brownsburg, Indiana, with his wife Amy; their three daughters, Jill, Emily, and Grace; a rabbit; and a sometimes-inside cat.

Brad would love to hear about your experiences with this book (the good, the bad, and the ugly). You can write to him at bradmiser@me.com.

Dedication

To those who have given the last full measure of devotion
so that the rest of us can be free.

Acknowledgments

A special thanks to Laura Norman, Acquisitions Editor extraordinaire, for involving me in this project. I appreciate the efforts of Keith Cline, Development Editor and Copy Editor, for ensuring the content of this book is meaningful and does allow you to learn iTunes in 10 minutes and for transforming my gibberish into readable text. Thanks to Jennifer Kettell, the Technical Editor who made sure this book is accurate and "tells it like it is." And Kristy Hart and Lori Lyons deserve kudos for the difficult task of coordinating all the many pieces, people, and processes that are required to make a book happen. Last, but certainly not least, to the rest of the important folks on the team, including Cheryl Lenser, Cindy Teeters, Nonie Ratcliff, San Dee Phillips, and the rest of the top-notch Sams staff, I offer a sincere thank you for all of your excellent work on this project.

We Want to Hear from You

As the reader of this book, *you* are our most important critic and commentator. We value your opinion and want to know what we're doing right, what we could do better, what areas you'd like to see us publish in, and any other words of wisdom you're willing to pass our way.

You can email or write me directly to let me know what you did or didn't like about this book—as well as what we can do to make our books stronger.

Please note that I cannot help you with technical problems related to the topic of this book, and that due to the high volume of mail I receive, I might not be able to reply to every message.

When you write, please be sure to include this book's title and author, as well as your name and contact information. I will carefully review your comments and share them with the author and editors who worked on the book.

Email: consumer@samspublishing.com

Mail: Greg Wiegand
            Associate Publisher
            Sams Publishing
            800 East 96th Street
            Indianapolis, IN 46240 USA

Reader Services

Visit our website and register this book at informit.com/register for convenient access to any updates, downloads, or errata that might be available for this book.

Introduction

Apple's iTunes is an amazing application that enables you to obtain, store, organize, and enjoy music, movies, TV shows, podcasts, books, and other digital content. You can play this content on your computer, and you can stream it to other devices over a network. If you have an iPod, iPhone, or iPad, iTunes is the essential companion software that you use to move your content and information onto your device. iTunes is a very powerful and feature-rich application; this book will help you quickly learn to take advantage of all that iTunes offers.

About This Book

Similar to the other books in the *Sams Teach Yourself in 10 Minutes* series, the purpose of this book is to enable you to learn how to use iTunes quickly and easily; hopefully, you'll even enjoy yourself along the way! This book is composed of a series of lessons. Each lesson covers a specific aspect of using iTunes. For example, Lesson 4, "Listening to Music," teaches you how to find and play music in your iTunes Library while Lesson 11, "Streaming Music with AirPlay," shows you how to stream music and other content from your computer to other locations.

The lessons generally build on each other starting with the more fundamental topics covered in the earlier chapters and moving toward more advanced topics in the later chapters. iTunes isn't a completely linear application so there are a few cases where you'll find references to later lessons within a lesson. In general, if you work from the front of the book toward the back, your iTunes education will progress smoothly.

The lessons include both information and explanations along with step-by-step tasks. You'll get more out of the lessons if you perform the steps as you read the lessons. Figures are included to show you what key topics look like on your computer's screen.

Who This Book Is For

This book is for anyone who wants to get the most out of iTunes; iTunes is a well-designed application, but even so, you'll learn much faster with this guide to help you. If you've never used iTunes, this book can get you started and help you move towards becoming an iTunes guru. If you've dabbled with iTunes while using an iPod or iPhone, this book will help you go beyond basic syncing and be able to use all of iTunes' amazing functionality. If you've spent a fair amount of time using iTunes, this book will provide lessons to round out your iTunes expertise.

What Do I Need to Use This Book?

The only technical requirement to be able to use this book is a computer with iTunes installed on it (don't worry, if iTunes isn't installed, this book shows you how to download and install it too). Some iTunes' functionality requires an Internet connection, so you'll have a much better experience if you can connect your computer to the Net.

In addition to the basic technical requirements, you just need a sense of adventure and curiosity to explore all this book offers you. iTunes is a fun application to use and, with this guide to help you, it should be fun application to learn as well.

Conventions Used in This Book

Whenever you need to click a particular button or link or make a menu selection, you'll see the name of that item in **bold**, such as in "Click the **Music** tab to configure your music sync settings." You'll also find three special elements (Notes, Tips, and Cautions) throughout the book.

> NOTE: A note provides information that adds to the knowledge you gain through each lesson's text and figures.

> TIP: Tips offer alternate ways to do something, such as keyboard shortcuts, or point out additional features of which you can take advantage.

CAUTION: You won't find many of these in this book, but when you do come across one, you should carefully read it to avoid problems or situations that could cause you grief, time, or money.

Is This Book a PC or a Mac?

iTunes is available for computers running the Windows operating system and for Macs; it works almost identically on each type of computer. Therefore, this book is for people using PCs and for those who have a Mac. When there are differences between iTunes running under Windows and iTunes on a Mac, you'll see those differences noted. For example, since Macs and PCs use slightly different keyboards, most of the keyboard shortcuts are different and you'll find the shortcut for each computer explained.

You'll also see figures for each type of computer in this book. If you happen to be using a Mac and a figure shows the PC version of iTunes, it will look a little different than your version of iTunes, but the information provided by the figure (and text) is just as applicable to you as to a PC user. This works in the other direction too; if you use a PC and see a figure captured on a Mac, the iTunes interface will look a little different, but the functionality is the same.

LESSON 1

Getting Started with iTunes

In this lesson, you gain a high-level overview of iTunes to understand its major interface elements, its key functionality, and the general steps you perform in almost every task. You also learn how to install iTunes and to ensure you are using the most current version. Finally, you learn how to tweak the iTunes window.

Touring iTunes

Understanding iTunes' general functionality and user interface helps you as you learn to perform specific tasks throughout this book. In this section, you learn what iTunes can do, how the application window is organized, and the general steps involved in many common tasks.

Knowing What iTunes Can Do

iTunes can do many things, some obvious and some not so obvious. To whet your appetite for iTunes, check out the following list to see just some of what awaits you:

- ▶ Use the iTunes Store to preview, purchase or rent, and download music, movies, TV shows, podcasts, books, apps, and more.

- ▶ Create a library to store and organize music that you import from audio CDs, download from the iTunes Store or other online sources (such as Amazon.com), or import from elsewhere on your computer.

▶ Listen to the music you've stored in iTunes. With iTunes, you can quickly find the specific music you want to listen to and then easily control how that music plays.

▶ Build, organize, and watch a video collection that includes TV shows, movies, music videos, and more. You can obtain videos from the iTunes Store, you can import them from DVDs, and you can add videos stored elsewhere on your computer. Once they are in your Library, iTunes makes watching video content fun and easy.

▶ Tag (label) your iTunes content so that you can expertly find and organize it.

▶ Create playlists containing the specific songs you want to hear in the order you want to hear them or create smart playlists that are based on a set of criteria, such as all the jazz music you have rated at four or five stars. Smart playlists collect and organize content for you automatically, whereas you configure the contents of standard playlists manually.

▶ Subscribe to and enjoy podcasts, both audio and video.

▶ Manage the content on and customize your iPod, iPhone, iPad, or Apple TV.

▶ Share your music collection with other people over a wired or wireless network; you can also listen to music other people share with you.

▶ Burn your own music CDs to play in one of those "ever-more difficult to find" CD players. (Perhaps you still have one in your car, as part of a boom-box, or in your home stereo setup.) You may also want to back up your iTunes content to data CDs or DVDs.

▶ While this list covers a lot of tasks, there's much more you can do. For example, use Ping to connect with others about your iTunes activities and to see what other people and your favorite artists are up to. Convert audio and video into different formats. Use iTunes built-in back-up functionality to protect your investment (time and money). iTunes is a feature-rich application.

As you can see, iTunes offers many features for your audio and video enjoyment, all packaged in one powerful, yet easy-to-use application.

Understanding the iTunes Window

The iTunes application uses a single window that is organized into panes. On the far left is the Source pane, where you choose the source of content or the device you want to use. Across the top and bottom of the iTunes window are the controls you use to play content, get information about what's happening, find content, and open and close panes. The largest pane, just to the right of the Source pane, is the Content pane, where you see the contents of whatever is selected in the Source pane. At the far right of the window, you may see the iTunes sidebar; you can open or close this as you see fit. Another optional pane is the Item Artwork and Video Viewer pane that appears at the bottom of the Source pane when it is open. (You can open or close this pane, too.)

NOTE: **One Window?**

Stating that iTunes uses only one window is not precise. Almost all the time you see just one window, which the iTunes window shown in Figure 1.1. Like most applications, iTunes can have other windows open. One of these is the Equalizer, which you learn about later in this book. You can also open playlists in their own windows. A third window is the Multiple Speakers window that appears when you use AirPlay to stream your iTunes content to other devices.

Choosing the Source

The Source pane is the starting point for almost every task you do in iTunes. That's because it is where content sources and devices you work with are organized. When you select an item in the Source pane, its contents appear in the Content pane, where you can view and work with them or the controls you use to work with the item appear (such as the settings you use to configure iPod syncing). The Source pane has several different sections; each section has different types of sources.

FIGURE 1.1 The iTunes window is organized into a number of panes, configurable to suit your preferences.

You learn how to work with each of these sources through the lessons in this book. For now, it will be useful as you move ahead if you have a general idea about the sources available to you.

The LIBRARY contains all the content you are managing in iTunes. This content is organized by type, with an icon representing each, as follows:

▶ Music

▶ Rentals

▶ Movies

▶ TV Shows

▶ Podcasts

- ▶ Books

- ▶ Apps

- ▶ Ringtones

- ▶ Radio

Some of these categories, such as Rentals (which contains content you've rented from the iTunes Store), appear only after you have added content of that type to your Library. There are also preferences you learn about later that enable you to hide or show categories.

NOTE: **How Does iTunes Know?**

iTunes uses the file type for content files to place them within the various categories in the Library, such as Music or Movies. It also uses the Media Kind tag, which you'll learn about in Lesson 7, "Tagging iTunes Content." You can change the category where content is stored by changing its Media Kind tag.

The STORE is where you go to access the iTunes Store and to browse content you've purchased. The Store source contains the following icons:

- ▶ iTunes Store

- ▶ Ping

- ▶ Purchased playlists (exists only after you've purchased content from the iTunes Store)

NOTE: **Playlists**

Playlists are customized collections of music, video, and other content in your iTunes Library. (Think of a playlist as a custom CD without the disc itself or the storage limitation of a disc.) You can create your own playlists, and iTunes creates some playlists for you automatically or based on criteria you provide. Playlists don't actually contain any content; instead, they contain pointers to content stored in the Library.

The DEVICES source contains icons (when you have the related devices connected to your computer) for the hardware devices you use, including the following:

▶ Apple TV

▶ iPods

▶ iPhones

▶ iPads

▶ CDs

The Genius tool chooses music that "goes with" music you are currently listening to or a song that you select. The Genius is a good way to listen to your music in new ways or to rediscover music in your Library that you haven't heard in awhile. The GENIUS source contains:

▶ Genius

▶ Genius Mixes

▶ Genius playlists that you save

The PLAYLISTS section contains the following:

▶ iTunes DJ

▶ Playlists

▶ Folders containing playlists

Browsing and Viewing Content

The largest pane of the iTunes window is the Content pane. In this pane, you see the contents of the source selected on the Source pane. You have many options for how the content appears, and each source can have its own Content pane configuration.

You can choose from among different views, show or hide the browser, change the information displayed, sort the lists, and so on. For example, compare Figure 1.1, which shows the Content pane for the Music source in the Cover Flow view, to Figure 1.2, which shows the same content in the Album List view.

FIGURE 1.2 Compare this figure to Figure 1.1 to see the Content pane in two different views.

When you select an icon in the LIBRARY or PLAYLISTS section, you see the contents that correspond to that icon. For example, you can browse the music in your entire Library or just within a playlist. To play a song, you select it in the Content pane and click the Play button. Or, you might drag a song onto a playlist icon in the Source pane to add it to that playlist.

If you select the iTunes Store source, you access the Internet and move into the iTunes Store.

When you select an iPod, iPhone, or iPad on the Source list, the controls you use to configure the select device appear instead of content.

As you work through the lessons in this book, you learn how to work with the Content pane for all the sources.

Controlling iTunes

Along the top and bottom of the iTunes window are controls you use to work with content, get information about what iTunes is doing, and so on. Other lessons in this book cover the details of each of these elements, so for now we'll just take a quick look at the elements that display so that you have a basic understanding about what they are. Starting at the top-left corner of the window and moving to the right, you see the following:

▶ **Playback controls.** Here, you see the familiar Rewind, Play/Stop/Pause, Fast Forward, along with the Volume slider. These work as you probably expect them to.

▶ **Information window.** In the center of the top part of the iTunes window is the Information window. This area contains a variety of information about what you are doing at any point in time. For example, when you are playing music, you see information about the music currently playing. When you import music, you see information about the import process. When you download music from the iTunes Store, you see information about the download process. You can change the information displayed in this area, as you'll learn later.

▶ **View buttons.** Click these buttons to change the view you are using for the Content pane. From left to right, they are List, Album List, Grid, and Cover Flow.

▶ **Search tool.** You use the Search tool to search for songs, podcasts, video, or other content in your Library.

NOTE: **Window Controls**

One difference between the Mac and Windows versions of iTunes is the location of the Window controls. In the Mac version, the three buttons (Close, Minimize, Zoom) appear in the upper-left corner of the window. In Windows version, the controls (Minimize, Maximize, Close) appear in the upper-right corner.

Moving from left to right along the bottom of the iTunes window, you see the following:

▶ **Add Playlist.** You use this button to create your own playlists.

▶ **Shuffle.** You use the Shuffle button to shuffle the tracks in the selected source so that they play in random order rather than in the order in which they are listed in the Source pane.

▶ **Repeat.** You use the Repeat button to cause tracks to repeat within a selected source. You can repeat them once or have them repeat continuously until you stop iTunes from playing them.

▶ **Show/Hide Item Artwork and Video Viewer pane.** Click this button, and the pane opens if it is closed or closes if it is open.

▶ **Source information.** Located at the center of the bottom of the window, this area provides information about whatever is selected on the Source pane, such as the number of items, total playing time, and disk space required to store the content being shown. This becomes especially useful at certain times, such as when you are burning a CD or building a playlist, because you can see how much storage space your selection requires (so you know if it will fit on one CD, for example).

▶ **Select speakers.** When you use an AirPlay network to stream content to other devices, you use this menu to choose the devices on which the content will play. You learn about AirPlay in Lesson 11, "Streaming Music with AirPlay."

▶ **Genius.** Clicking this button causes the Genius to create a playlist based on the song currently selected in the Content pane.

▶ **Show/Hide the iTunes sidebar.** Click this to open or close the iTunes sidebar.

NOTE: **Changing Buttons**
Some of the buttons you see are contextual, meaning they appear only when a source to which they apply is selected. For example, if you select the Podcasts source, the Genius button doesn't appear because the Genius works only on music.

Using the Item Artwork or Video Viewer Pane

This pane, which opens under the Source pane, can either display album artwork associated with the song currently playing or the song currently selected or you can use it to watch video. As you learned earlier, you can hide or show this pane.

When you work with music or other audio content, it displays the associated artwork. For example, in Figure 1.3, you see the album art associated with the song currently playing.

FIGURE 1.3   As I was writing this lesson, music from *The Lord of the Rings* soundtrack was playing.

When you work with video content, this pane becomes the Video Viewer, in which you can watch that video. (You can view it at a larger size, too, as you'll learn later.)

If you click the pane, it opens in a separate window. When you hover over the window, you see controls and information about the content playing or a static image if you have it set to display the selected content. You learn more about this pane in Lesson 4, "Listening to Music," and in Lesson 6, "Watching Video."

Working with Ping

Ping is an iTunes social networking feature that you can use to follow artists and to see what other people are listening to, purchasing from the iTunes Store, and so on. If you are familiar with Facebook, you'll find Ping pretty similar, except that it is focused on music and is tied into the iTunes Store. You can use Ping from within the iTunes Store or in the Ping pane, which, when shown, appears along the right side of the iTunes window. You learn about Ping in Lesson 14, "Going Further with iTunes."

Learning the iTunes Way

Now that you have a good understanding of what appears in the iTunes window, you should know that all tasks you do with iTunes include the following two general steps:

1. Find the content or device you want to use for the task. To do this, you first select the source in the Source pane where the content is stored (or organized, as in the case of playlists) or the icon representing the device you want to use. For example, if you want to listen to music, select **Music** or click a playlist; if you want to sync an iPod, select its icon on the list. The content of whatever you select appears in the Content pane; you can then browse that content, or you can search it to find the specific items you want to use, such as songs that you want to listen to. In the case of an iPod or other device, the Content pane fills with the controls you use to configure and sync the device.

2. Use iTunes controls to perform the task. You can use the playback controls to listen to music or watch video, set the sync controls to configure how information is moved on to an iPad or other device, and so on.

Just about every task you do with iTunes follows this pattern: Select a source and find the content you want to work with, and then use the iTunes controls to do what you are trying to do. After you've worked through the next couple of lessons, this pattern will become second nature to you.

Installing iTunes

Of course, to be able to use iTunes, the application must be installed on your computer. If your computer already has iTunes installed, you can skip this section and move directly to the next one (where you learn how to make sure you are using the current version of iTunes).

If your computer doesn't have iTunes on it, follow these steps to download and install it:

1. Open a web browser.

2. Go to http://www.apple.com/itunes/download/ (see Figure 1.4).

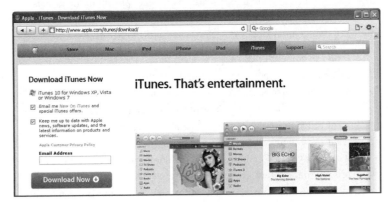

FIGURE 1.4   Downloading iTunes from the Apple website is straightforward.

3. Check or uncheck the two check boxes to suit your preferences. These check boxes add you to mailing lists related to iTunes. If you check one or both of them, you must provide your email address before moving to the next step.

4. Click **Download Now**.

5. If you use a Windows PC, follow the onscreen instructions to download and install iTunes. If you use a Mac, a disk image will be downloaded to your computer; when that's done, move to the disk image, double-click the iTunes Installer, and follow the onscreen instructions.

TIP: **Launching iTunes**
You can open iTunes in a number of ways. On a Windows PC, the installer (by default) installs an iTunes icon on your desktop, and of course, you can always launch it through the Start menu or in any other usual way you open applications. On a Mac, the iTunes icon

is installed on the Dock by default, so you can launch it by clicking its icon, you can double-click the application's icon in the Applications folder, and if you open an audio file, iTunes launches (if set to with a preference). If you connect an iPod, iPhone, or iPad to either kind of computer, iTunes launches automatically (or comes to the front if it is already open).

Updating iTunes

Like other applications, iTunes is updated regularly to address bugs, improve features, and so on. Because iTunes is a free application, updates are also free, so there's no reason not to be using the most current version. You can update iTunes manually, or even better, you can configure it to check for updates automatically.

Here's how to check for updates manually:

1. Open iTunes.

2. On a Windows PC, choose **Help, Check for Updates**. On a Mac, choose **iTunes, Check for Updates**. The application checks your version of iTunes against the current version.

3. If you are using the current version, click **OK** to clear the dialog telling you so. If you aren't using the current version, you're prompted to download and install it. Follow the onscreen instructions to download and install the newer version.

NOTE: **Updating iTunes on a Mac**
When you update iTunes on a Mac (manually or automatically), the operating system uses the Software Update application, just as it does for other Apple applications. If an update is found when you check for updates manually, the Software Update application launches and then downloads and installs the update.

Here's how to configure iTunes to check for updates automatically:

1. Open iTunes.

2. On a Windows PC, choose **Edit, Preferences**. On a Mac, choose **iTunes, Preferences**. The Preferences dialog opens.

3. Click the **General** tab (see Figure 1.5).

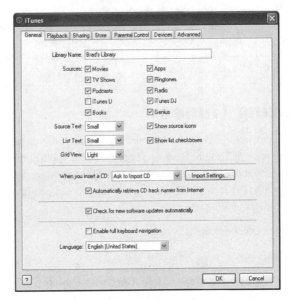

FIGURE 1.5   To ensure you are always using the current version, configure iTunes to check for updates automatically.

4. Check the **Check for new software updates automatically** check box.

5. Click **OK**. The dialog boxes closes. When iTunes finds a new version, you're prompted to download and install it.

Configuring the iTunes Window

Most of the time, you configure the way the Content pane appears when you are working with a specific source, which you learn about in Lesson 4. However, you can use some settings to configure more general aspects of the iTunes window. To configure these options, open the General tab of the Preferences dialog as described in the preceding section and shown in Figure 1.5.

On the General tab, you can configure the following appearance-related options:

▶ **Show check boxes.** These check boxes determine whether the associated categories appear under the LIBRARY section of the Source pane. If a check box is checked, the category's icon appears, and you can access content of that type. If it is unchecked, the icon does not appear on the Source pane, which means you can't access the content it represents. When you uncheck a check box associated with content you have in your Library, such as Podcasts, the content itself (podcasts in this example) remains in your Library. To view and listen to the hidden content, simply check the Podcasts check box again.

▶ **Source Text menu.** This menu toggles the relative size of the text you see next to items on the Source pane between Small or Large. Try each setting to see which you prefer.

▶ **List Text menu.** This menu toggles the relative size of the text you see on lists in the Content pane between Small or Large. Again, try each setting to see which you prefer.

▶ **Grid View menu.** When you select **Light** on this menu and view the Content pane in Grid view, its background is white. If you select **Dark**, the background becomes black.

▶ **Show source icons check box.** This check box determines if you see icons next to each item on the Source pane (checked) or not (unchecked).

▶ **Show list checkboxes check box.** In list views, the check box next to each track determines whether the track is active. If you play a source with inactive tracks, those tracks are skipped. You can also use this to configure other actions, such as if a track has to be active to be included in a smart playlist or included when you sync an iPod. If the Show list checkboxes check box is not checked, the check box doesn't appear, so you can't use it to make tracks active or inactive. If the check box is checked, you can activate or inactivate individual tracks.

NOTE: **Appearance Settings in This Book's Illustrations**
The screenshots you see throughout this book are configured with the settings shown in Figure 1.5. If you configure iTunes on your computer differently, your screen might look somewhat different, but the information you learn will be just as applicable.

Summary

In this lesson, you took a tour of iTunes to gain a general understanding about how the application is organized, to familiarize yourself with its major features, and to learn the general steps you perform as part of all tasks. You learned how to install iTunes and to make sure you are using the most current version. You also learned how to change the look of the iTunes window. In the next lesson, you learn how to use the iTunes Store.

LESSON 2

Working with the iTunes Store

In this lesson, you learn how to gain access to the iTunes Store, which is integrated into iTunes making it convenient to add audio and video content to your Library. You learn how to set up and use an iTunes Store account, configure Store settings, browse and search for content, and what the implications are of digital rights management for your content.

Touring the iTunes Store

The iTunes Store is a great way to add content to your iTunes Library. Many types of content are available in the Store, including the following:

- ▶ Music
- ▶ Music videos
- ▶ Movies (rent and purchase)
- ▶ TV shows (rent and purchase)
- ▶ Applications for iPhone, iPods, and iPads
- ▶ Podcasts
- ▶ Audiobooks

You can preview any content in which you are interested before you purchase it, and there is a fair amount of free content available for you. And, unlike physical CDs or DVDs, you can pick and choose content you purchase, such as individual songs or TV episodes.

The best part is that the iTunes Store is fully integrated in iTunes, so shopping there is easy. The Store enables you to browse for content by clicking graphics or text links. And you can search for specific content of interest to you. When you purchase content, it is downloaded immediately to your Library and includes a number of tags so that it is placed into the correct categories automatically.

In addition to enabling you to purchase audio, video, and other types of content, the iTunes Store offers a number of other features, such as the following:

- ▶ **Ping.** Ping is the iTunes social network through which you can connect with artists and other iTunes users.

- ▶ **iTunes gift cards.** iTunes gift cards are available in many retail stores and in various amounts. Redeeming a card requires just a few steps.

- ▶ **Gifts.** You can easily give iTunes content to other people.

- ▶ **Genius recommendations.** The iTunes Store's Genius feature makes recommendations to you based on your previous purchases and based on items you've indicated that you like. This is a good way to discover new music, movies, and TV shows.

- ▶ **Wish list.** You can add items to your wish list to collect items you are interested in without purchasing them.

- ▶ **Alerts.** You can sign up for alerts to be notified when new music from specific artists is available.

- ▶ **Complete my album.** This feature enables you to purchase the rest of the songs on an album after you've downloaded one or more individual songs from it.

To access the iTunes Store, you click its icon in the Source pane. Depending on a preference setting, the Store either fills the Content pane or the entire iTunes window, as shown in Figure 2.1. Along the top of the Store window, just below the iTunes controls, is the main menu bar. At the far left are navigation controls. Starting with the Home button (the house icon) and moving toward the right, you see menu selections for the various types of content available, such as Music, Movies, and so on. At the far right is the Account button, which you use to access your iTunes Store account.

FIGURE 2.1   The iTunes Store is integrated into iTunes, making shopping there a seamless experience.

There are two basic ways to find content in the Store: browsing and searching. Anything inside the Store window is a live link, including text titles, graphics, and "top lists." You can browse around the Store by clicking any links you see. You can search the iTunes Store using the Search tool at the top-right corner of the iTunes window or through the Power Search tool.

Once you find specific content, you can preview it, read information about it, see reviews from others, see related content, and purchase or rent it (movies or TV shows), as shown in Figure 2.2.

FIGURE 2.2   Here, you see an album page where you can get more information about the album, preview its content, and purchase individual songs or all of them.

To move from the iTunes Store back to your iTunes Library, you either close the store by clicking its Close button or make another selection in the Source pane.

Working with an iTunes Store Account

To be able to purchase content from the iTunes Store, you need to have an iTunes Store account. You also need an account to be able to download some of the free content, such as applications for an iPod or iPhone. Fortunately, obtaining an account is free. If you already have an Apple ID (the same one you use to make purchases at the online Apple Store) or an AOL account, you can use your existing account information in the iTunes Store.

Once you have an account, you can sign in or sign out and use the Store account tools to manage your account, such as to change some of your information or to review your purchase history.

Obtaining an iTunes Store Account

Like other iTunes Store functions, you can obtain an account directly from within iTunes. To obtain and sign in to an iTunes Store account, just complete the following steps:

1. Open iTunes.

2. Click **iTunes Store** in the Source pane (see Figure 2.3). iTunes connects to the Internet and you move into the iTunes Store.

FIGURE 2.3   Click its link in the Source pane to move to the iTunes Store.

3. Click **Sign In** in the upper-right corner of the iTunes window, as shown in Figure 2.4. The Sign In dialog appears (see Figure 2.5).

NOTE: **No Sign In Link?**

If you see a username rather than the Sign In button, iTunes is already logged in to an iTunes Store account. If the account is yours, skip the rest of these steps. If the account isn't yours, click the account shown and click **Sign Out** in the resulting dialog box so that you can create your own account.

FIGURE 2.4 The Sign In link enables you to sign in to an existing account or to create a new one.

FIGURE 2.5 Use this dialog to sign in to an existing account or to create a new one.

4. Click **Create New Account**. You move to the first screen in the account-creation process, as shown in Figure 2.6.

5. Read the information and click **Continue**. You move to the next screen in the process.

Welcome to the iTunes Store

Preview, buy, and download the latest music, movies, TV shows, apps, and more.

Start shopping on iTunes as soon as you've created your Apple ID. Click Continue to begin.

Cancel   Continue

FIGURE 2.6 You're guided through the account-creation process with information to read and forms to complete.

6. Read the information on each screen and follow the onscreen instructions to create an Apple ID. You'll provide your contact information, a credit card, and other information.

After you complete process, you receive your Apple ID and password and are ready to use this information to sign in to the iTunes Store.

Signing In to Your iTunes Store Account

You need to sign in to your iTunes Store account only once. From that point forward, iTunes remembers your account information unless you specifically log out. Signing in is easy:

1. Click the **Sign In** link.

2. Enter your Apple ID and password as shown in the Figure 2.7, or if you have an AOL account, click the **AOL** radio button and enter that information instead.

3. Click **Sign In**. You sign in to your iTunes Store account and are ready to use it.

FIGURE 2.7   You just need an Apple ID or AOL account username and password to log into the iTunes Store.

CAUTION: **Signing Out of Your Account**

If you use iTunes on a computer to which other people have access and leave yourself logged in to your account, anyone who uses your computer can purchase content (especially if you have enabled iTunes to remember your password for purchasing). To protect your account, you can sign out of it by clicking the **Account** button, which shows your Apple ID or AOL account name when you are logged in to your account. The Sign In dialog box appears; click **Sign Out**. The Account button is labeled Sign In, indicating you are no longer signed in; then, someone needs to know your account name and password to be able to access your account, making it a much safer situation for your wallet.

Viewing and Updating Your iTunes Store Account

Times change, and sometimes so does your personal information, such as your address or the credit card you want to use in the iTunes Store. If such changes occur in your life, you can change your Apple ID account information. You can also view information about your account, such as purchase history. You can access your account information as follows:

1. Click your iTunes Store account name as you do when you want to sign out of your account. The Sign In dialog box appears.

Because you are already logged in, you don't see the Create New
Account button; now you see the View Account button.

2. Enter your password.

3. Click **View Account**. You see the Apple Account Information
   screen.

On the Apple Account Information screen, various buttons enable you to
change your account information and to manage aspects of your account,
including the following:

▶ To change your account information (such as your address), click
  the **Edit Account Info** button and follow the onscreen instructions to change your information. For example, you can use this
  screen to change your password to protect access to your
  account.

▶ To change your credit card information, click **Edit Payment
  Information** and follow the onscreen instructions to change your
  credit card information.

▶ You can change the country or region your account is associated
  with by clicking **Change Country or Region**. This is an important aspect of your account because the iTunes Store functions
  differently and offers content based on your country or region.

▶ To view your purchase history, click the **Purchase History** button.
  The screen shows a detailed list of all the transactions for your
  account, as shown in Figure 2.8. You can review the list, filter it to
  show specific dates, and move between pages of information.

▶ If you click **Manage Allowances**, which appears after you set it
  up by clicking Buy iTunes Gifts in the QUICK LINKS section of
  the iTunes Store Home page, you can create and assign an
  amount of credit someone will have in the iTunes Store on a
  monthly basis. This is a good way to enable someone to make
  purchases in the iTunes Store while controlling how much is
  spent. You can assign an allowance to an existing iTunes Store
  account or create a new one for someone and assign the
  allowance to it.

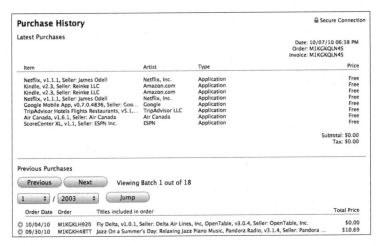

FIGURE 2.8 When you view your account, you can see the purchases you've made in the iTunes Store.

▶ The Ping section enables you to change your Ping profile and enable or disable Ping.

▶ Like other iTunes Store users, you can publish reviews of content available in the Store. Click the **Manage Reviews** button to "review" your reviews in case you change your mind.

▶ Alerts are email notifications about specific artists, such as when music from a specific artist is added to the iTunes Store. You add alerts for specific artists from the artist's page in the iTunes Store. Use the **Manage My Alerts** button to disable current alerts or to add alerts based on the content in your iTunes Library or that you've downloaded from the iTunes Store.

▶ iMixes are playlists that people publish in the iTunes Store. You can publish any playlist you create, and people who use the iTunes Store can see its contents. (Only music available in the iTunes Store can be included in an iMix.) To work with your iMixes or to learn how to create an iMix, click the **Manage iMixes** button (which appears after you publish a playlist as an iMix).

▶ If you have a web page or blog, you can add iTunes widgets to it to show your purchases, the artists you've downloaded the most, or your reviews. To get the HTML code for any of these widgets, click **Manage My iTunes**. Check the check box for the widgets you want. Click the **Get HTML Code** button to retrieve the widget's code to add to your web page or blog.

▶ When you perform certain actions in the iTunes Store, you see warning dialogs. If you check the option to prevent those from showing again, they no longer appear. You can reset all the warnings by clicking **Reset Warnings**.

▶ Click the **Terms of Service** button to display the current terms and conditions for the Store.

▶ To view Apple's privacy policy, click the **Privacy Policy** button.

When you finish working with your account, click **Done**. You return to the iTunes Store.

Setting iTunes Store Preferences

You can set a number of iTunes Store preferences to configure how you interact with it. To access these settings, open the Preferences dialog box and click **Store**, as shown in Figure 2.9.

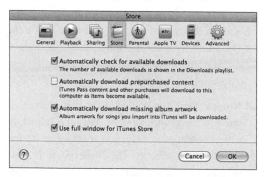

FIGURE 2.9 Configure various aspects of how the Store works with this pane of the Preferences dialog.

Check or uncheck the check box next to each item to enable or disable it. The options are as follows:

▶ **Automatically check for available downloads.** When this is enabled, iTunes automatically checks for downloads available to you, and you see their number next to the Downloads playlist. For example, you can buy a season pass for a TV series, which means that as soon as a new episode is released you can download it. When a download is available, you can click the **Downloads** option on the Source list and then download the content.

▶ **Automatically download prepurchased content.** If you do pre-purchase content, such as a season pass, this options causes that content to be downloaded automatically as soon as it becomes available in the iTunes Store.

▶ **Automatically download missing album artwork.** Music and other content has artwork associated with it; you see this artwork in various locations in iTunes and on other devices. It's better if you have as much artwork as possible because you see that art-work in the iTunes window when you use the Cover Flow view, the Artwork viewer, and so on. Having more artwork makes the iTunes window more interesting and enables you to identify con-tent more easily because you see the artwork associated with it. Any content you download from the iTunes Store has artwork automatically. With this option enabled, iTunes will download artwork for any music you have in your Library even if you didn't download it form the Store (such as music you imported from a CD). This only works for music available in the iTunes Store. (So if you import a CD that isn't available, iTunes won't be able to download its artwork.)

▶ **Use full window for iTunes Store.** With this option enabled, the iTunes Store fills the iTunes window. With it disabled, the iTunes Store fills the Content pane only; you continue to see the Source and other panes of the window. The iTunes Store is best used when it has plenty of screen real estate, so I recommend you enable this option unless you have a large display and use a very large display resolution. (Most of the screenshots in this book show the window in this configuration.) To move from the iTunes Store back to iTunes, you click the Close button, which is the X located on the far left of the iTunes Store menu bar.

Finding Content in the iTunes Store

The first step in downloading content from the Store is finding content of interest to you. There are two basic ways to do this: browsing or searching. Browsing is simple; you just click links you see until you find something of interest. Searching enables you to find specific content based on parameters you define. The method you use depends on what you are doing.

Browsing can be a great way to discover content you might be interested in but don't know about yet. You can click through the Store to explore in various ways; browsing can result in lots of great content of which you might not have even been aware.

Searching is better when you have some idea of what you are after. For example, you might want to find music by a specific artist or download a particular song. In such situations, searching is the way to go.

No matter what kind of content you are interested in (music, video, apps, and so on), the basic techniques to find that content are similar. You see examples for specific kinds of content in later lessons, but the following sections give you an overview of how to use each method.

Browsing the iTunes Store

To browse the Store, click **iTunes Store** in the Source pane. You move into the iTunes Store, as shown in Figure 2.10.

When you first enter the Store, you move to the Home page. You can return to this page at any time by clicking the **Home** button (house icon) on the iTunes Store menu bar, which appears just under the iTunes controls at the top of the window. The Home page provides an overview of the content available in the iTunes Store along with the QUICK LINKS area that contains links to specific tools or locations.

FIGURE 2.10   Browsing the iTunes Store is a great way to discover new content.

You can browse from the Home page by clicking any of the links you see, and just about everything is a link, including the text, graphics, items on the various lists you see, and so on.

If want to browse for a specific type of content, such as Movies, click its text button on the menu bar. The Home page for that content appears as shown in Figure 2.11.

TIP: **Menu Options**

If you click the downward arrow that appears when you point to a menu option, you see drop-down menus you can use to jump to specific categories of content, such as movie genres or HD TV.

You can browse these pages just as you can the iTunes Store Home page. Eventually, you "drill down" far enough to reach specific content you can then preview and download. (You'll see examples of this in later lessons.)

FIGURE 2.11   You can browse the Home page for types of content, such as the Movies Home page you see here.

NOTE: **Picking Up Where You Left Off**

iTunes remembers your location in the iTunes Store. If you move back into iTunes and then return to the Store, you come right back to the page you were viewing instead of moving to the iTunes Store Home page.

Searching in the iTunes Store

Browsing is useful, but it can be time-consuming and might not lead you to the content you want. When you want something specific, you can search using the iTunes Store's Search tools. There are two kinds of searches: basic search and power search.

When you do a basic search, you search by one search term. Basic searches are fast and easy, but can sometimes find a lot of content of little interest to you. When you perform a power search, you can combine several search terms to make searching more precise.

To perform a basic search, follow these steps:

1. Move into the iTunes Store.

2. In the Search tool, type the text or numbers for which you want to search. As you search, iTunes will present a list of potential search terms under the Search tool, as shown in Figure 2.12.

FIGURE 2.12   When you perform a basic search, iTunes suggests potential searches; click one to use it.

3. To perform a search using one of the searches iTunes suggested, click it on the menu or continue typing until you complete the search term, and then press **Enter** (Windows) or **Return** (Mac). The search results appear (see Figure 2.13).

4. To further refine the search, click one of the categories shown in the FILTER BY MEDIA TYPE box located on the left side of the window. For example, if you click Music, the results include only music.

5. Browse the search results until you find content you want to preview or download. (You see examples of this in later lessons.)

TIP: **Clear a Search**
To clear the search term, click the X button in the Search tool.

FIGURE 2.13 Search results can include many different types of content, such as music, movies, podcasts, and so on.

Sometimes a basic search doesn't find the results you want or it provides too many results that you have to wade through. Fortunately, you can use a power search if you want to find something very specific. With a power search, you can search by more than one attribute at the same time.

To perform a power search, move to the Home page and click **Power Search** in the QUICK LINKS section on the right side of the window. The Power Search tool appears, as shown in Figure 2.14.

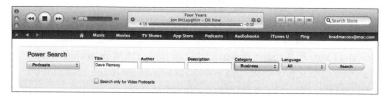

FIGURE 2.14 A power search enables you perform very specific searches.

TIP: **More Power Searching**

If a search doesn't yield the results you want, you can click the Power Search link on the results page to change the search parameters.

Use the menus and boxes to configure the search. When you choose a category on the far left side of the window, the rest of the fields adapt to the type of content you selected. Use the fields to complete the search criteria and click **Search**. The search results appear on a screen that looks like that shown in Figure 2.13. In Lesson 3, "Building Your iTunes Audio Library," you see how to use the Power Search tool to find specific music. Searching for other kinds of content is similar.

Understanding Digital Rights Management

Digital rights management (DRM) is way for publishers to protect their digital content from being copied and distributed without limits. Some of the content you download from the iTunes Store has DRM applied to it, and so you need to understand potential limitations of content that you obtain from the iTunes Store.

Fortunately, a lot of the content in the iTunes Store is not protected by DRM, and you don't have to worry about usage restrictions. Content without DRM is called iTunes Plus content. All the music currently available in the iTunes Store is iTunes Plus content, so you don't need to think about DRM for music you download. There are other kinds of iTunes Plus content, as well.

All other content, including music you purchased from the iTunes Store before iTunes Plus music was available or other DRM-protected content was removed, is protected, and you should be aware of the limitations imposed by DRM, which include the following:

▶ You can use protected content (except for rented content) on up to five devices at a time. This means you can play protected content on up to five computers at the same time. Note that this limit does not apply to iPods, iPhones, or iPads. You can use iTunes content on more than five of these devices.

▶ Rented content can be stored on only one device at a time. Also, rented content is deleted automatically after it has been stored on a device for 30 days. It is also deleted 24 hours after it is first played. (However, you can watch that content as many times as you like within the 24-hour period.)

▶ You can store content from up to five different iTunes Store accounts on the same device. This means you can transfer protected content downloaded from up to five different iTunes Store accounts onto one iPod, iPhone, or iPad. Content from more than five accounts will not be included in a sync.

▶ You can burn a playlist with protected music onto a CD seven times. This limit applies only to a playlist with exactly the same content. If you modify a playlist, such as by adding or removing songs, the limit counter is reset.

To enable a computer to play protected iTunes content, it must be authorized. This happens automatically when you download content through your iTunes Store account, and you can also manually authorize computers. You can also de-authorize computers as needed in case you would exceed the five-computer limit to play protected content on a sixth computer. Authorizing and de-authorizing computers is covered in Lesson 14, "Going Further with iTunes."

Summary

In this lesson, you learned how to prepare to take advantage of the iTunes Store to add content to your iTunes Library. You learned how to create and access your account, set iTunes Store preferences, browse and search the Store, and what protected content means. In the next lesson, you learn how to add music to your iTunes Library (with downloading music from the iTunes Store being just one of your options).

LESSON 3

Building Your iTunes Audio Library

In this lesson, you learn how to add music to your iTunes Library so that you can do lots of great things with it, such as tagging it, organizing it, sharing it, and, oh yeah, listening to it. There are a number of ways to get content into your Library: importing audio CDs, downloading music from the iTunes Store, downloading music from Amazon.com, and importing music files stored elsewhere on your computer.

Importing Audio CDs

Adding your audio CDs to your iTunes Library enables you to listen to them on your computer, add them to iPods/iPads/iPhones, and so on. Before you start importing CDs, however, take a moment to learn about and configure your import options. After you've set the options you want to use, you'll be ready to import your CDs.

To configure your import settings, complete the following steps:

1. Launch iTunes by double-clicking its application icon, choosing it on the Windows Start menu, or clicking it on the Mac's Dock.

2. Choose **Edit**, **Preferences** (Windows) or **iTunes**, **Preferences** (Mac). The Preferences dialog appears, as shown in Figure 3.1.

> TIP: **Opening Preferences**
> You can open the Preferences dialog box on a Windows PC by pressing **Ctrl+,** and on a Mac you press **Cmd+,**.

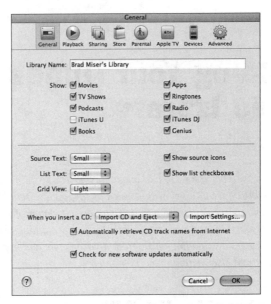

FIGURE 3.1   The General tab of the iTunes Preferences dialog enables you to configure options for importing audio CDs, among other things.

NOTE: **Other On CD Insert Options**

The other options on the When You Insert a CD menu can be useful. After you've imported all of your CDs, select the **Ask to Import CD** option so that you don't accidentally import the same CD twice. Select the **Begin Playing** option if you want CDs to play automatically without importing them. If you don't want iTunes to take any action, select **Show CD**.

---

3. Click the **General** tab.

4. On the When you insert a CD menu, choose **Import CD and Eject**. As you can probably tell, this option causes iTunes to automatically import a CD as soon as you insert it into your computer. When the import process is complete, the disc is also ejected automatically. This is the best option for importing a large number of audio CDs quickly.

5. Ensure the **Automatically retrieve CD track names from Internet** check box is checked. (It is checked by default.) When you insert a CD into your computer, iTunes will connect to CD databases on the Internet to identify CDs you insert by title, artist, and song names. In addition to displaying this information when you listen to a CD, iTunes automatically adds this information to your imported music.

NOTE: **Other On CD Insert Options**

The other options on the When You Insert a CD menu can be useful. After you've imported all of your CDs, select the **Ask to Import CD** option so that you don't accidentally import the same CD twice. Select the **Begin Playing** option if you want CDs to play automatically without importing them. If you don't want iTunes to take any action, select **Show CD**.

---

6. Click **Import Settings**. You use these settings to select the type of audio file formats into which iTunes will convert your audio CDs, as shown in Figure 3.2.

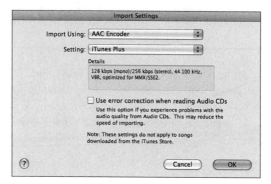

FIGURE 3.2 Use the Import Settings dialog to configure how iTunes imports music from audio CDs.

When you convert music from a CD into digital form for the iTunes Library, there is always a trade-off between file size and quality. The higher quality of encoder you choose, the larger the resulting files are, which means you can fit fewer songs on portable devices, such as iPods. You want to choose an option that provides a good balance between quality and file size.

6. On the Import Using drop-down menu, choose **AAC Encoder**. This is the best setting in most cases because it produces high-quality music files with relatively small sizes. The encoder options are listed in Table 3.1 in case you want to check out the other options.

TABLE 3.1   Encoding Options

Encoder File Format	When to Use
AAC	Most of the time (unless you have a specific reason to use one of the others).
AIFF	You want to be able to use the music in another application.
Apple Lossless	You demand the maximum quality in music playback and file size is not important. (Perhaps you don't use a portable device to listen to your music.)
MP3	You only use portable devices that don't support AAC.
WAV	You need audio content in this older format for a specific purpose, such as to be able to import into another application.

7. On the Setting drop-down menu, choose **iTunes Plus**. This is the best selection in most cases because it provides really good-quality audio. Table 3.2 shows other options. After you select a setting, the properties of that setting are shown in the box under the menu.

TABLE 3.2   Setting Options

Encoder File Format	When to Use
iTunes Plus	Most of the time (unless you have a specific reason to use one of the others).
High Quality	You accept less quality of encoding for smaller file sizes.

TABLE 3.2 Setting Options

Encoder File Format	When to Use
Spoken Podcast	The audio content you are importing is in spoken form, such as audiobooks.
Custom	You want to tweak the options. When you select this, you are presented with an additional dialog that you can use to set Stereo Bit Rate, Sample Rate, and other technical aspects of the encoding process.

8. Click **OK**. The Import Settings dialog closes.

9. Click **OK**. The Preferences dialog closes, and you're ready to import your CDs.

TIP: **Not All Settings Are Equal**

You don't have to use the same settings for the all the CDs you import. For example, you might choose AAC and iTunes Plus for audio CDs, but use AAC and Spoken Podcast when you import audiobooks.

After you've configured the import process, actually importing audio CDs is a snap. Assuming you've selected the Import CD and Eject option, just insert a CD into your computer. iTunes connects to the Internet, identifies the CD, selects it on the Source list, and starts the import process. The track currently being imported is marked with an orange circle; tracks that have been imported are marked with a green circle, as shown in Figure 3.3. At the top of the iTunes window, you see detail about the import process, such as the song currently being imported and the current import speed.

Depending on the computer you are using, you can expect the import process to be many times faster than the playing time of the disc. When the process finishes, iTunes plays an alert sound and ejects the disc (again, assuming you've selected the Import and Eject option).

FIGURE 3.3 While a CD is being imported, the import status of each song is indicated by a colored icon and you see information about the import process at the top of the iTunes window.

NOTE: **iTunes Does Multitasking**

You can use iTunes for other tasks while it is importing music. For example, you can select and play music already in Library while you are importing new content.

Insert the next CD and so on until you've imported all the CDs that you want to have in your iTunes Library.

Downloading Music from the iTunes Store

As you learned in Lesson 2, "Working with the iTunes Store," the iTunes Store is a great place to obtain music and other audio content. Because the iTunes Store is integrated into iTunes, downloading music from the Store is simple.

NOTE: **Assumptions, Assumptions**

For this section, I assume you've worked through Lesson 2. This means you have an iTunes Store account and are familiar with how to navigate around the Store, to browse it, and so forth. I also assume you've configured your preferences so that the Store fills the iTunes window.

Searching is a great way to find specific music you want to buy. (You download music in the same way regardless if you searched for it or browsed around the Store for it.)

1. Select **iTunes Store** on the Source list. The Store fills the iTunes window, and you move to the iTunes Store Home page.

2. Click the **Power Search** link in the QUICK LINKS section located along the right side of the Home page.

3. To limit your search to a specific kind of content, choose it on the pop-up menu. For example, choose **Music** to search for music. The Search tool updates to include fields appropriate for the kind of content for which you are searching.

4. Enter the information for which you want to search, such as Artist, Song, Genre, and such, as shown in Figure 3.4. You can make your search more or less specific by entering more or less information.

FIGURE 3.4   Using the iTunes Store's Power Search is a great way to get to specific music that you want to add to your iTunes Library.

5. Click **Search**. Items that meet your search criteria display in the lower parts of the window. The results are organized into logical

collections based on the type of content for which you searched.
For example, when you search for music, you see albums, songs,
and music videos. In each category, you see information appropriate for that category, such as the Songs category in which you
see name, album, artist, and so on for each song.

6. To preview content, move the pointer over it and click the **Play**
    button that appears; where it appears depend on what you hover
    over. When you hover over a song, the Play button replaces the
    track number; when you hover over video, the Play button
    appears in the lower-right corner of the thumbnail. When you
    click the Play button, a 90-second preview plays. (If you preview
    a music video, it appears in a separate preview window.)

7. When you want to purchase and download content, click its **BUY**
    button. This button can include different information depending
    on the screen it appears on. It always shows the price of the con-
    tent. It can also describe what you are buying. For example,
    when you are previewing a music video, the button is labeled
    BUY VIDEO.

8. If prompted, enter your account's password and click **Buy** or just
    click the **Buy** button depending on the prompt you see. Figure
    3.5 shows an example. The content you purchase is downloaded
    to your computer and added to your iTunes Library.

FIGURE 3.5 Use this dialog to confirm you want to make a purchase from
the iTunes Store.

TIP: **Easier Purchasing**

If you check the **Remember password** check box in the Sign In dialog or the **Don't ask me about buying again** check box in the purchase confirmation dialog, when you click **Buy** buttons in the
future, content is purchased immediately. This is convenient, but
you don't get a chance to reconsider (as you do when you have to
enter your password before you buy).

Content you purchased is automatically collected in the Purchased playlist.
(You learn more about playlists in Lesson 8, "Creating and Using
Playlists.") Select that playlist on the Source list and you'll see the content
you've downloaded from the iTunes Store, as shown in Figure 3.6.

FIGURE 3.6   Content you download from the iTunes Store is automatically
collected in the Purchased playlist.

TIP: **More Than Buy**

If you click the downward-facing arrow to the right of the Buy buttons, you see a menu with various commands, such as Gift, which enables you to give the content to someone else, share via Facebook, and so on. One option enables you to add content to your wish list, much like a shopping cart where you can store content you might be interested in purchasing later; after you add content to your wish list, you can move back to it by clicking **My Wish List** in the QUICK LINKS section of the iTunes Store Home page. From your wish list, you can preview or purchase content.

Downloading Music from Amazon.com

Amazon.com offers a huge selection of music that you can purchase, download to your computer, and add to your iTunes Library. Amazon also provides an application that will automatically add music you purchase to your iTunes Library for you, making music from Amazon.com almost as convenient as music from the iTunes Store.

First, download and install the Amazon MP3 Downloader application on your computer:

1. Using a web browser, go to **Amazon.com**.

2. From the Music, Movies & Games menu, select **MP3 Downloads**.

3. Click the **Install the Downloader** option on the menu at the top of the MP3 Downloads window.

4. Click **Download Now**.

5. Follow the instructions to install the application on your computer.

NOTE: **More than Amazon**

Other web sites offer music you can download and add to your iTunes Library. Most of these don't offer an application that automatically adds your download to iTunes like Amazon does. If not, you need to add the content using the Add to Library command covered later in this lesson.

> **NOTE: Amazon.com's Music Format**
>
> As you can tell, all of Amazon.com's music is in the MP3 format. Although this is an older format, it provides good quality at reasonable file sizes. iPods, iPhones, and iPads can play MP3 music, and you can listen to it from within iTunes, so there's not much downside to having music in this format in your iTunes Library.

After you have installed the Downloader, you can shop for and purchase music from Amazon.com:

1. Using a Web browser, move to **Amazon.com**; open the **Digital Downloads** menu along the left side of the window, and choose **MP3 Downloads**. You move into the MP3 Store.

2. Browse or search for music of interest to you.

3. To preview music, click the **Play** button to the left of a song you want to hear.

4. To purchase and download music, click the **Buy MP3 album** button as shown in Figure 3.7 or click the **Buy MP3** button to download an individual song. As in the iTunes Store, you can purchase individual songs or entire albums.

5. Confirm your purchase at the prompt.

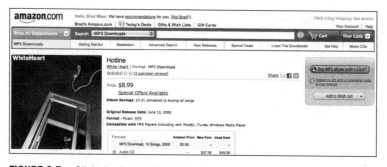

FIGURE 3.7 Click the Buy MP3 button next to music you want to purchase and download from Amazon.com.

The Amazon MP3 Downloader application opens, and the music
you purchased downloads to your computer, as you can see in
Figure 3.8. By default, the application also adds your music to
your iTunes Library.

FIGURE 3.8   The Amazon MP3 Downloader application downloads music
from Amazon.com and adds it your iTunes Library.

6. When the Downloads Complete prompt appears, click **OK**.

The music you purchased is now in your iTunes Library where you can
listen to it, add it to playlists, move it to an iPod, and so on.

TIP: **Skipping a Step**

If you don't want to be prompted when the download process ends,
check the **Don't show this message again** check box. When future
downloads complete, you don't have to take any action.

Importing Audio Files Already Stored on Your Computer

You can also add audio files that are stored on your computer to your iTunes Library. For example, if you download audio files from a website, you have to add those files to the iTunes Library to be able to work with them using iTunes.

To add an audio file stored on your computer to the iTunes Library, complete the following steps:

1. In iTunes, choose **File**, **Add File to Library** (Windows) or **File**, **Add to Library** (Mac).

2. Move to and select the file you downloaded.

3. Click **Open** (Windows) or **Choose** (Mac), shown in Figure 3.9. The content will be copied into your iTunes Library.

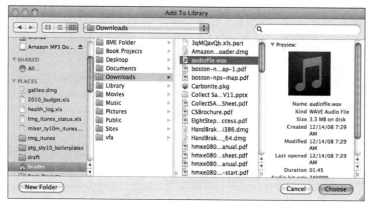

FIGURE 3.9   You can add any audio file on your computer to your iTunes Library.

4. Use iTunes **Info** tools to tag the content you've added, such as naming it, putting it in a genre, and so on. Unlike music you purchase from the iTunes Store or Amazon.com, most audio files you add from other sources won't be labeled with the information you need to be able to find and use it easily, so you need to

tag the content manually. You learn more about the iTunes Info tools in Lesson 7, "Tagging iTunes Content."

TIP: **Converting Audio Content**

If you want to change the format of music or other audio content in your iTunes Library, such as changing a WAV audio file you downloaded from the Web into an AAC file, you can use iTunes Convert tools. These are explained in Lesson 14, "Going Further with iTunes."

Summary

In this lesson, you learned how to add music to your iTunes Library from several sources. You learned how you can import any audio CD into iTunes. You also saw how easy it is to purchase and download music from the iTunes Store and Amazon.com. Lastly, you learned how to add audio files stored on your computer. In the next lesson, you learn how to listen to all the great music stored in your iTunes Library.

LESSON 4

Listening to Music

In this lesson, you learn to use iTunes to listen to the music in your iTunes Library; iTunes offers lots of great listening tools that enable you to enjoy your music when and how you want to. After setting a few audio preferences, you learn how to find music by browsing or searching in your Library. You also learn about the many ways you can configure the iTunes window and, of course, how to control your tunes.

Setting Audio Playback Preferences

You can use iTunes Playback preferences to control some aspects of how your music plays. You can take advantage of these features by using the Playback pane of the iTunes Preferences dialog box. To access this pane, choose **Edit**, **Preferences** (Windows) or **iTunes**, **Preferences** (Mac). Then click the **Playback** tab.

On this pane, you can configure the settings described in the following list and shown in Figure 4.1:

▶ **Crossfade.** This effect causes one song to fade out and the next one to fade in smoothly, eliminating the gaps of silence between songs. To activate it, check the **Crossfade Songs** check box and use the slider to set the amount of fade time. If you move the slider to the left, songs fade out more quickly. If you move the slider to the right, songs overlap; as one song starts to fade out, the next starts to fade in and you hear them both at the same time.

▶ **Sound Enhancer.** This effect is the iTunes effect that "adds depth and enlivens" the quality of your music. The actual result of this effect is a bit difficult to describe, so the best thing to do

is try it for yourself. Check the **Sound Enhancer** check box and
use the slider to set the relative amount of enhancement. Play
music for a while. If your music sounds better to you, increase
the amount of the effect. Keep increasing it until the music starts
to sound worse to you. Then, reset it to the level that sounded
good to you. If you prefer your music unenhanced, uncheck the
check box.

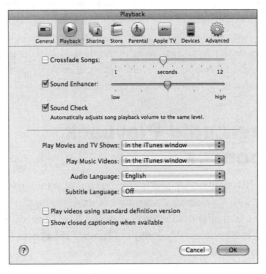

FIGURE 4.1   Use the Playback preferences to configure how audio sounds.

▶ **Sound Check.** iTunes enables you to set the relative volume
   level of songs, meaning you can make them play louder or qui-
   eter than other songs. The Sound Check check box sets the relative volume level of all songs to be the same. To implement this
   effect, check the **Sound Check** check box. (You learn how to
   change the relative volume level of songs in Lesson 7, "Tagging
   iTunes Content.")

After you've configured the Playback preferences, click **OK** to save your
changes and close the dialog box.

> NOTE: **More on Crossfade**
>
> This Crossfade setting does not impact audio CDs when you play them in iTunes. Because there is a physical gap between tracks on the CD, iTunes can't do anything about it. The Crossfade setting applies to other sources, such as your Library and playlists.
>
> Some music, such as live recordings, doesn't have gaps between tracks, but instead its tracks are meant to play in one "stream." If you enable Crossfade, this can make the music sound odd because instead of applause between tracks, they fade together. To get back to the way the tracks are supposed to play, you can override the Crossfade setting for specific music. You learn how to do this in Lesson 7.

Viewing the Content Pane

As you learned earlier, the Content pane is where you see and work with the contents of items on your Source list, such as your music or TV shows. There are many ways to change how information appears in the Content pane, and you can even have different views for different sources. For example, you might want to view your music in one way, but want to see your TV shows listed in a completely different way.

Working with Lists

iTunes stores lots of information, called tags, about the content in your Library. Examples of tags for music include the following:

- ▶ Genre
- ▶ Artist
- ▶ Album
- ▶ Name
- ▶ Rating
- ▶ Last Played

These are just a few examples; there are many other tags available to you. Over time, you learn which tags are useful to you and which aren't. (You learn how to configure the tags for your content in Lesson 7.)

In the iTunes window, tags appear as columns. You can choose which tags you see in the window for specific sources, and you can use tags to sort and organize the Content pane. The order in which items appear in the Content pane is important because it can determine the order in which they play. You can use the Content pane in its default state, or you can customize it to make finding and working with content easier and faster for you.

In the next section, you learn about the many ways you can configure the Content pane to browse your music. Most of these show lists of tracks, with the rows being the individual songs and the columns displaying the tags about those songs. Figure 4.2 shows an example.

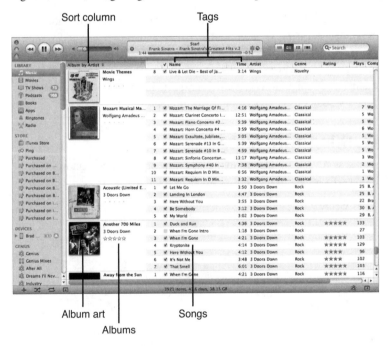

FIGURE 4.2 Over time, you learn which tags are the most useful to you and how you want the Content pane to appear.

You can change how lists of songs appear in a number of ways, including the following:

- ▶ **Change the sort column.** If you click a column heading, the list is sorted by that tag; the column by which the window is currently sorted is highlighted in a light gray box. You can change the order of the sort by clicking the triangle that appears at the right edge of the current sort column. When the triangle points up, the list is sorted in descending order; when it points down, the list is sorted in ascending order. The sort order is important because it determines how the songs are listed for viewing purposes and it determines the order in which they play (unless you use the Shuffle feature to make the play order random).

- ▶ **Choose column options.** Some column headings are menus from which you can choose grouping or other options. When you click such column headings, the menu appears and you choose the option you want. In Figure 4.2, the far left column is the Album tag, which as you can see displays the album art associated with the songs being displayed. If you click the column heading, you see different ways to group the songs, including Album by Artist, Album by Title, and Album by Artist/Year; you can also change the size of the album art in the column.

- ▶ **Change column widths.** If you hover over the right edge of a column heading so that the pointer changes to a vertical line with an arrow coming out each side, you can drag the edge of the column to change its width. Making a column smaller enables you to display more tags in the window without scrolling but also displays fewer of the tags in the column.

- ▶ **Reorganize columns.** If you click and hold down on a column heading, you can drag it to a new location in the Content pane. This enables you to organize the columns in an order that you find most useful.

- ▶ **Change the columns that appear.** When you work with a specific source, you can determine which columns (tags) appear on this list. You do this through the View Options dialog, which you can access by choosing **View, View Options**. The View Options dialog box appears, as shown in Figure 4.3. In the upper-left corner, you see the source for which you are configuring view options. (In this figure is a folder called Rock, which is a way to organize playlists. You learn about this in Lesson 8, "Creating and Using Playlists.") Each tag is listed along with a check box. To show a tag (column) in the Content pane, check its check box. To hide a tag, uncheck its check box. When you have configured the source, click **OK**. The dialog closes and the Content pane displays the columns whose check boxes are checked.

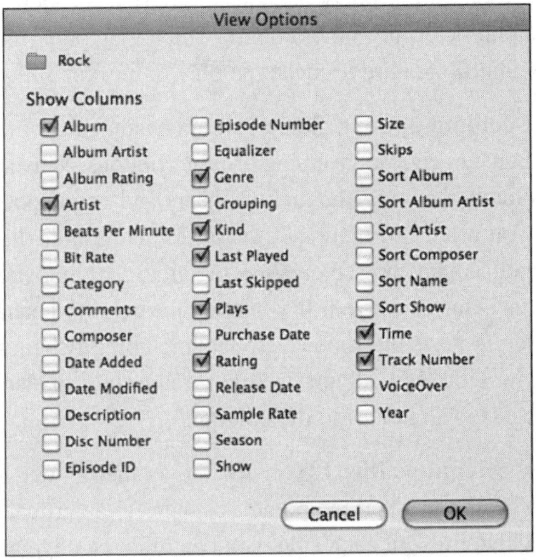

View Options

Rock

Show Columns

☑ Album	☐ Episode Number	☐ Size
☐ Album Artist	☐ Equalizer	☐ Skips
☐ Album Rating	☑ Genre	☐ Sort Album
☑ Artist	☐ Grouping	☐ Sort Album Artist
☐ Beats Per Minute	☑ Kind	☐ Sort Artist
☐ Bit Rate	☑ Last Played	☐ Sort Composer
☐ Category	☐ Last Skipped	☐ Sort Name
☐ Comments	☑ Plays	☐ Sort Show
☐ Composer	☐ Purchase Date	☑ Time
☐ Date Added	☑ Rating	☑ Track Number
☐ Date Modified	☐ Release Date	☐ VoiceOver
☐ Description	☐ Sample Rate	☐ Year
☐ Disc Number	☐ Season	
☐ Episode ID	☐ Show	

Cancel   OK

FIGURE 4.3   Use the Playback preferences to configure how audio sounds.

TIP: **Where Are Those Columns?**

If more columns are displayed than will fit in the iTunes window, columns you add may be off to the right where you can't see them. You can scroll to the right to see them using the scrollbar at the bottom of the window or make the window larger. Of course, you can move the most useful columns toward the left of the window so that they display where you want them to.

Using the Column Browser

The Column Browser enables you to quickly move to specific music by making selections in columns; each selection narrows the content displayed so that you can quickly focus on the music of interest to you. Like the options you learned about earlier, the Column Browser can be configured for each source, and its settings are stored for that source so that you can use them each time you work with that source.

The Column Browser has a number of configuration options. You can choose the columns it displays, and you can have it appear at the top of the Content pane or along the left side.

You can configure the Browser using the following steps:

1. Enable the Browser by choosing **View, Column Browser, Show Column Browser**.

2. Set the Browser's location by choosing **View, Column Browser, On Top** or **View, Column Browser, On Left**.

3. Now configure the columns you want to see in the Browser by choosing **View, Column Browser, *Columnname***, where *Columnname* is the name of the column you want to display. Columns you select to display are marked with a check mark.

4. Repeat step 3 to display all the columns in the Browser that you want to see. The columns available to you depend on the source selected on the Source pane.

5. To have compilation albums grouped together as an album rather than by artist, choose **View, Column Browser, Group Compilations** to mark that option with a check mark.

NOTE: **Compilation Albums**

Compilations are albums based on some criteria other than artist. For example, Greatest Songs of the Best Movies of 1985 could include songs from different artists and different soundtrack albums. If you don't have iTunes group compilations, the songs from such an album are scattered throughout the Content pane based on the artist and source. This can make finding this kind of music difficult. If iTunes groups compilations, they appear as an album even though the album includes different artists and sources.

6. To group albums by the Album Artist tag, choose **View, Column Browser, Use Album Artists.**

NOTE: **Album Artists**

Some albums contain work credited to more than one artist, such as an Elvis album that contains one song that is a collaboration between Elvis Presley and Wolfgang Amadeus Mozart. When iTunes displays such albums, it separates the tracks based on the artist and shows two albums, one by Elvis Presley and another by Elvis Presley and Wolfgang Amadeus Mozart. The Album Artist tag enables you to assign an artist tag to music for browsing purposes without changing the artists credited with that music. If you do this, you can enable the Browser to group music by album artist instead of the credited artist, which is the default grouping tag. This displays the music grouped by the album artist so that it appears together.

To use the Browser, make selections in each of its columns. As you work toward the right (when the Browser is on the left) or down (when the Browser is on top), the content shown narrows based on your selections. The Browser enables you to quickly find specific music via browsing as long as you know the major tags associated with the music you want to find.

TIP: **Show or Hide the Browser Quickly**

To show the Browser if it is hidden or to hide it if it is shown, press Ctrl+B (Windows) or Cmd+B (Mac).

Figure 4.4 shows an example using the Browser on the Music source, with the Column Browser being displayed on the left and the Genre, Artists, and Albums columns shown. I've selected Rock as the genre so that only artists with rock music in my Library are shown in the Artists column.

To further narrow my browsing, I selected Switchfoot in the Artists column. This causes only albums with Switchfoot as the artist to be shown in the Albums column. Because All is selected in the Albums column, the window is showing all the albums in my Music library from the group Switchfoot in the rock genre. I could have further narrowed my browsing by selecting a specific album on the list. In that case, only songs on the selected album would appear on the list.

FIGURE 4.4 The Column Browser enables you to browse music quickly to find songs you want to work with.

NOTE: **Browser Columns**

Like other columns, you can resize the columns in the Browser. Unlike other columns, you can't sort by them or change their order.

The list you see to the right of or below the Browser (depending on where you set the Browser to appear) works just like you learned in the previous section. You can scroll it, change its columns, sort it, reorder the columns, and so on. Using the Browser, you can quickly narrow the contents on the list to make finding music easier.

> TIP: **Browser Size**
>
> If you position the Browser at the top of the window, you can change its size relative to the content list by dragging its Resize handle (the dot in the center of the bar separating the Browser from the list) up or down.

Figure 4.5 shows the Column Browser on top and with the same selections as in Figure 4.4.

FIGURE 4.5   Here, the Column Browser is displayed at the top of the window. (Compare this to Figure 4.4 where it is displayed on the left.)

The location and options for the Browser are retained with each source. So, when you select that source, the last configuration of the Browser is used. You might find the Browser more useful for some sources than others, and over time, you'll find the settings that make it work most efficiently for you.

Browsing for Music

Browsing for music is a good way to find music you want to listen to, add to a playlist, and so on. As you've seen, you can browse a source by selecting it and using the list of contents and the Browser to view the music in the source. iTunes also provides different views of content so that you can change how you browse using the tools you just learned about.

The four views are as follows:

- ▶ List
- ▶ Album List
- ▶ Grid
- ▶ Cover Flow

Each of these options has benefits, so experiment with them until you find the views that work best for you.

To choose a view, click one of the **View** buttons shown in Figure 4.6 or choose a view from the View menu.

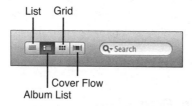

FIGURE 4.6 Change the way in which content appears by choosing a view.

NOTE: **Views and the Browser**
You can show the Browser in the List or Album List view. The Browser is hidden in the Grid and Cover Flow views.

Browsing in List View

In many ways, List view is the simplest view but also one of the most useful. It presents the contents of the selected source in a list that works as you learned earlier in this lesson. You can use the Browser with the List view to make narrowing the list down even faster.

The List view is one of the most efficient views, and you can use it to browse to any content in your Library quickly, especially if you show the Browser. The only downside to the List view is that it lacks any visual pizzazz.

Browsing in Album List View

As you might expect from its name, the Album List view also presents a list, but it also groups the list of contents by the albums from which the content comes. Figure 4.5 shows an example of the Album List view. If you click the first column heading in this view, you see a menu that contains additional sort options (such as Sort Album by Title or Sort Album by Artist) and that enables you to change the size of the album art being shown (Small, Medium, or Large). You can also use the Browser to further refine your browsing.

Like the List view, Album List view enables you to browse to any content quickly, and it includes your album artwork, making it a more appealing view visually. Also, grouping content by albums makes finding specific content a bit easier than in the List view. The drawback to this view compared to the List view is that the album groups take up more space than the straight list, so you can't see as much content in the Content pane without scrolling.

Browsing in Grid View

In the Grid view, content is organized in thumbnails, with each thumbnail representing the content being browsed organized by album, artist, genre, or composer. You choose the type of organization you want by clicking one of the four buttons (Albums, Artists, Genres, or Composers) at the top of the window. Drag the Size slider located at the right side of the window to increase or decrease the size of each thumbnail. Figure 4.7 shows the Grid view with the Genres option selected.

FIGURE 4.7 The Grid view is useful when you are most interested in group-ings of songs instead of browsing for individual songs.

You can't use the Browser with this view; if you show the Browser, you move into the List view.

The Grid view can be useful when you aren't interested in seeing any detail about the music you are browsing and don't want to see individual songs. (You can see only the groups you are working with, not the contents of those groups.)

Following are some pointers about using the Grid view:

▶ If you move the pointer across a thumbnail, you scroll through the album art for the content included in the group.

▶ When you hover over a thumbnail, the Play button appears. Click this to play the content in the group.

▶ If you perform a secondary (right) click on the Albums, Artists, or Composers buttons, you can choose the Group command. This command causes the thumbnails to be grouped appropriately. For example, if you choose Group Composers, the thumbnails are grouped by composer name; if you click at the start of a group, you see how many composers and songs are in the group.

> ▶ If you perform a secondary click on the Albums button, you can
>   use the Sort Albums menu that appears to choose how the albums
>   are sorted in the window.

Browsing in Cover Flow View

The Cover Flow view represents your music as though you are flipping
through a stack of CDs. When you choose this view, the Content pane is
organized in two sections. In the top section, you see the album art associated with the content selected on the Source pane. The album art directly
facing you is the album in focus, and you see its name and artist under the
album cover, and its contents are at the top of the list in the lower part of
the window. As you select albums, the contents of the list change to reflect
the album currently in focus.

The Cover Flow view is both useful and visually appealing, and it just
might be the most fun view to browse because you can browse music
quickly, but you also get a lot of information about individual songs in
the list.

Figure 4.8 shows an example of the Music source in the Cover Flow view.

The Cover Flow view is very useful, as you can see:

> ▶ You can "flip" through the "stack" of CDs in several ways. You
>   can drag the scrollbar to the left or right; the faster you drag, the
>   faster you flip. You can also click the arrow at either end of the
>   scrollbar. And, you can click any of the album art you can see to
>   jump to that album.

> ▶ The order in which the list is sorted determines the order in
>   which the album art is shown. For example, if you click the
>   Artist column heading, the album art in the upper part of the
>   view is sorted by artist; whereas if you click the Album heading,
>   the covers are sorted by album.

> ▶ Like other views, you can browse in the Cover Flow view while
>   listening to music. After you are inactive for a few seconds, the
>   stack flips so that the album currently playing moves back into
>   focus.

FIGURE 4.8   The Cover Flow view is a great way to view information about individual songs while seeing your album art in all its glory.

▶ You can play an album by double-clicking its cover.

▶ If you perform a secondary (right) click on an album cover, you see a pop-up menu. From this menu, you can jump to the song currently playing, rate the current song if you jump to it (you learn about rating in a later lesson), change how the content is sorted (this does the same thing as clicking one of the column headings), reverse the current sort order, and change the size of the text shown under each album.

▶ To change the relative size of the sections, drag the **Resize** handle, which is located just below the center of the scrollbar, up or down to increase or decrease the size of the art compared to the number of songs shown on the list.

▶ You can work with the list in the lower part of the view, just like the list described earlier. For example, you can change the size of columns, reorder columns, and so on. You can scroll the list using the vertical scrollbar.

▶ When you click a song on the list, the album from which that song comes into focus.

▶ If you don't need to see any other application or document windows open on your computer except iTunes (playing music is all you are using your computer for at the moment), showing the Cover Flow view in full screen is kind of cool. To do this, click the **Full Screen** button located to the right of the album scrollbar. The upper part of the Cover Flow view fills the screen, and you don't see the list. You can browse in this mode, and you can use the playback tools in the lower-left corner to control your music. You can control volume using the slider just to the right of the scrollbar. An example is shown in Figure 4.9. To return to the standard iTunes window, click the **Full Screen** button again or press the **Esc** key.

FIGURE 4.9   The Cover Flow view in Full Screen mode enables you to see your album artwork at a large size and use all the tools the Cover Flow view offers.

Searching for Music

At times, you want to find specific content quickly. To do this, you can use the iTunes Search tool located in the upper-right corner of the window. You can search for music (and other content) by any of the following criteria:

▶ All

▶ Artist

▶ Album

▶ Composer

▶ Song

To search for music, perform the following steps:

1. Select the source you want to search. (For example, click the **Music** source to search your entire music collection.)

2. If you want to search by a specific criterion, click the **magnifying glass** icon located at the left edge of the Search tool; if you want to search on all categories, skip to step 4.

3. Choose the criterion by which you want to search, such as **Artist**.

4. Type the data for which you want to search in the Search tool. As you type, iTunes searches the selected source and presents the songs that meet your criterion in the Content pane. It does this on-the-fly, so the search narrows with each keystroke. As you type more text or numbers, the search becomes more specific.

5. Keep typing until the search becomes as narrow as you need it to be to find the content in which you are interested. For example, the search shown in Figure 4.10 has found all versions of the song "Ghost Riders in the Sky" in my library.

To clear a search, click the **Clear** button (X) that appears in the Search tool after you have typed in it.

FIGURE 4.10   Searching is a quick way to get to specific music.

Listening to Music

So far, you've learned how to find music by browsing and searching. Of course, one of the reasons you want to find music is to listen to it. iTunes offers many ways to listen to the music in your Library.

Controlling Music Within the iTunes Window

The first step in listening to music is to find the music you want to listen to. Earlier in this lesson, you learned how to browse and search for music; in later lessons, you learn how to use playlists and other tools to find music to listen to. Once you find the music you want to listen to, use the primary playback controls in iTunes as shown in Figure 4.11 and described in the following list to control your tunes:

▶ Select the song you want to hear and click the **Play** button in the upper-left corner of the window; select **Controls**, **Play**; press the spacebar; or just double-click the song. It begins to play. As the song plays, a Speaker icon appears next to it on the list in the Content pane (if a list is visible), and information about that song appears in the Information window at the top of the iTunes window (more about this important tool later in this lesson).

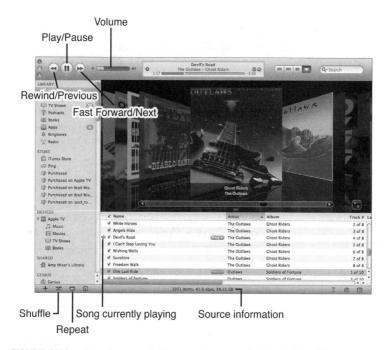

Volume
Play/Pause
Rewind/Previous
Fast Forward/Next

Shuffle ─┐ │ Song currently playing   Source information
Repeat

FIGURE 4.11 If you've listened to music on any device before, iTunes play-back controls are probably familiar to you.

NOTE: **Speaker Icon: More Than You Might Think**

When a song is playing, its Speaker icon has waves radiating from it to show it is playing. When you pause, the Speaker icon remains to show it is the current song, but the waves go away to let you know the song isn't currently playing.

▶ Control the volume of the sound by dragging the Volume slider to the left to turn it down or to the right to turn it up. You can also control the volume by selecting **Controls**, **Increase Volume** or **Controls**, **Decrease Volume**.

▶ To pause a song, click **Pause**; select **Controls**, **Pause**; or press the spacebar.

NOTE: **Crank It Up**
Using the Volume slider within iTunes only changes the volume of iTunes relative to your system's volume. If you can't make the music loud or quiet enough, adjust your system's volume level.

▶ When a song is playing and you click and hold the **Rewind** or **Fast Forward** button, the song rewinds or fast-forwards until you release the button.

▶ If a song is not playing or a song is playing but you single-click (but don't hold the button down) the **Rewind** or **Fast Forward** button, the previous or next song, respectively, is selected. You can also select **Controls**, **Next** or **Controls**, **Previous** to move to the next or the previous song.

▶ As you learned earlier in this lesson, you can change the order in which songs play by sorting the list of songs you are playing.

▶ For a little variety, you can have iTunes play songs in a random order using the Shuffle command. To use this feature, click the **Shuffle** button or choose **Controls**, **Shuffle**, **Turn On Shuffle**. The songs are reordered in the Content pane and play in the order in which they are listed (hopefully in a random fashion). The Shuffle button is highlighted in blue to indicate that it is active. You can choose how song are shuffled by choosing **Controls**, **Shuffle** and then choosing **By Songs**, **By Albums**, or **By Groupings**. If you choose one of the last two options, iTunes plays all the songs in the album or grouping in the order they appear and then select another song or grouping to play. To return playing order to its previous state, click the **Shuffle** button or choose **Controls**, **Shuffle**, **Turn Off Shuffle**.

▶ You can also have iTunes repeat music. To repeat all the music in the selected source until you stop playing music, choose **Controls**, **Repeat**, **All** or click the **Repeat** button once. The Repeat button becomes blue to show you that it is active, and the source repeats. To repeat only the current song, select **Controls**, **Repeat**, **One** or click the **Repeat** button a second time. The numeral 1 appears on the Repeat button to indicate that only the current song will be repeated. To turn off the repeat function, choose **Controls, Repeat, Off** or click the **Repeat** button until it is no longer highlighted in blue.

▶ You can prevent a song from playing by unchecking its check box. When that song's turn comes, it is skipped. To cause the song to play again, check its check box.

It might not seem like much, but the Information window in the center of the top of the iTunes window is actually quite powerful. It presents information about what is happening at any point in time and changes to reflect what you are doing.

> NOTE: **Listening to CDs**
>
> All the techniques for browsing, searching, and playing music work for CDs, too. Just insert the CD into your computer and select it from the Source list.

When music is playing, you see information about that music, such as the song name, artist, and album of the currently playing song. You also see a Timeline showing the total length of the song currently playing, as shown in Figure 4.12.

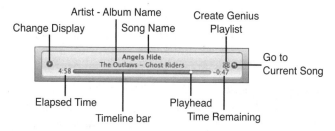

FIGURE 4.12 The Information area might not be much to look at, but there's a lot of information and control here.

The Playhead indicates the relative position of the music you are hearing at any point in time compared to the total length of the song. The time shown at the left end of the Timeline is always the time position of the Playhead, which is the amount of time the song has been playing. As a song plays, the Playhead moves to the right; the portion of the Timeline representing the amount of song that has been played is shaded (everything to the left of the Playhead).

The value shown on the right end of the Timeline can be either the total time of the track or the track's remaining time (indicated by a negative value). You can choose the value that is displayed by clicking the time; if total time is shown, it will becomes the remaining time and vice versa.

If you click the **Go to Current Song** button, the song currently playing is selected in the Content pane and is highlighted in blue. You might find this handy when you are working with other music sources while listening to a song because you can click this button to quickly return to the song that is playing.

If you click the **Change Display** button, the display changes to the next option, which depends on what you are doing. When you are listening to music, the display becomes a graphical representation of the volume levels at various frequency groups, as shown in Figure 4.13. You can return to the song information by clicking the button again.

Create Genius Playlist

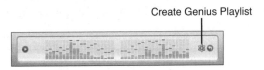

FIGURE 4.13   Okay, so it isn't that useful, but this graphic display is kind of cool looking.

TIP: **Going Backward**

To return to content you've recently played, choose **Controls, Play Recent**, and then choose the song, movie, playlist, or other content you want to hear from the list of the 10 most recent items you've played.

These are only two of the displays you see here. When you add music to your Library, the information and tools in the window become those you use for the import process. Likewise, when you burn a CD, the information shown is relevant to that process. When you sync an iPod, iPhone, or iPad, you see information about that process here. You can always cycle through the displays by clicking the **Change Display** button until the information you want to see appears.

Lastly, you can click the **Create Genius Playlist** button to create a new Genius playlist based upon the current song. You learn about the Genius in Lesson 8.

> NOTE: **Controlling iTunes with Keys**
>
> Some keyboards, such as those on MacBook Pros, have keys pre-programmed to control some iTunes functions, such as Play/Pause, Rewind, and so on. These are useful because iTunes doesn't have to be the active application to control your music. If you use a programmable keyboard, considering programming such basic commands on keys so that you can control iTunes without actually moving into the application.

Controlling Music with Your Keyboard

Using the onscreen controls is good, but you can also use keyboard shortcuts listed in Table 4.1 to make controlling music more convenient and faster.

TABLE 4.1   Keyboard Shortcuts in iTunes

Action	Windows Keys	Mac Keys
Play or pause	Spacebar	Spacebar
Start the current song over	Enter	Return
Fast forward in a song	Ctl+Alt+Right Arrow	Cmd+Option+Right Arrow
Rewind in a song	Ctl+Alt+Left Arrow	Cmd+Option+Left Arrow
Go to the next song in the source	Right Arrow	Option+Right Arrow
Go to the previous song in the source	Left Arrow	Option+Left Arrow
Go to current song	Ctl+L	Cmd+L
Increase volume	Ctl+Up Arrow	Cmd+Up Arrow

TABLE 4.1 Keyboard Shortcuts in iTunes

Action	Windows Keys	Mac Keys
Decrease volume	Ctl+Down Arrow	Cmd+Down Arrow
List view	Ctl+Shift+3	Option+Cmd+3
Album List view	Ctl+Shift+4	Option+Cmd+4
Grid view	Ctl+Shift+5	Option+Cmd+5
Cover Flow view	Ctl+Shift+6	Option+Cmd+6

Controlling Music with the Mini Player

Sometimes you might not want the iTunes window to take up so much screen space. This is where the Mini Player comes in. In this mode, the iTunes window shrinks to just include the basic playback controls and Information area, as shown in Figure 4.14.

FIGURE 4.14 The Mini Player provides access to key controls and information you need to listen to music while taking up little screen space.

TIP: **Always Show the Mini Player**

To make the Mini Player always stay on top of all open windows so that it is always visible, open the **Advanced** tab of the Preferences dialog box and check the **Keep Mini Player on top of all other windows** check box.

To switch to the Mini Player, choose **View**, **Switch to Mini Player** or press Ctl+M (Windows) or Shift+Cmd+M (Mac). You can use the Resize handle in the lower-right corner to make the Mini Player smaller; you can drag it all the way to the left to make the window so small that the only part of the iTunes window showing is the area to the left of the Information area, so you see only the playback controls. You can make it larger to view more information in the Information area.

To restore the iTunes window to its previous size, click the **Maximize** button (Windows) or **Zoom** button (Mac) or press Ctl+M (Windows) or Shift+Cmd+M (Mac).

TIP: **More Ways to Control on a Windows PC**

On a Windows PC, you can configure iTunes so that its icon displays in the System Tray. (Use the Advanced tab of the Preferences dialog box to do this.) Once configured, you can right-click the iTunes **System Tray** icon to access a variety of iTunes commands.

TIP: **More Ways to Control Music on a Mac**

If you perform a secondary (right) click on the iTunes Dock icon, you see a menu of commands you can use to control your music. You can also use the iTunes widget installed by default on the Mac's Dashboard.

Using the Item Artwork Viewer

As you learned during your iTunes tour in Lesson 1, "Getting Started with iTunes," the Item Artwork and Video Viewer pane shows the artwork associated with selected or currently playing music (and other content, for that matter). This is pretty nice, but it does more than just that.

To show this pane, click the **Show/Hide Item Artwork/Video Viewer pane** button, which is directly to the right of the Repeat button at the bottom of the window. The pane opens up into the Source pane, as shown in Figure 4.15. It shows either the artwork associated with either the song currently playing or the song currently selected. You can tell which it is by the text at the top of the pane, which will be either Now Playing or Selected Item. You can toggle between these two views by clicking that text.

FIGURE 4.15 There's more to the Item Artwork Viewer than meets the eye.

If you click the pane, it becomes a separate window that you can move around your desktop. When you hover over the window, you see playback controls you can use. These are similar to those in the iTunes window, as you can see in Figure 4.16.

FIGURE 4.16   When it is a separate window, you can also control your music in the Artwork Viewer.

TIP: **Multiple Viewers**

You can open multiple Artwork Viewer windows at the same time. Put the Viewer in Selected Item mode (click the Now Playing text at the top of the pane if Selected Item isn't there), and then click it to open a new window. Repeat this process as many times as you want.

Using the Equalizer

iTunes includes an Equalizer that you can use to adjust how your music sounds. To access the Equalizer on a Windows PC, choose **View, Show Equalizer**. On a Mac, choose **Window, Equalizer**. The Equalizer appears in a separate window, as shown in Figure 4.17. On the pop-up menu, you can choose an Equalizer preset, such as Bass Booster, which takes effect immediately, and your music is adjusted according to the Equalizer's settings. You can also make adjustments manually using the sliders and create your own presets.

FIGURE 4.17 To really customize your music, use the iTunes Equalizer.

NOTE: **The Visualizer**
iTunes includes a Visualizer that plays graphic effects onscreen. The movement of these effects is tied to the music playing; if you play music with a faster beat, the effects have quicker movements and vice versa. To explore the Visualizer, choose **Show Visualizer** from the View menu. You can choose different graphic effects by choosing **View, Visualizer** and then choosing the effect you want to use. You can have the Visualizer fill the screen by choosing **View, Full Screen**. To exit the Visualizer, press the **Esc** key.

Summary

In this lesson, you learned how to enjoy the great music in your iTunes Library. You learned how to set iTunes listening preferences. Then, you learned how to find music you want to listen to by browsing and searching. Once you found music you wanted to listen to, you learned how to control your tunes. In the next lesson, you learn how to add video content to your iTunes Library so that you can enjoy that, too.

LESSON 5

Building Your iTunes Video Library

In this lesson, you learn how to build up the video content in your iTunes Library by downloading video from the iTunes Store, adding content from DVDs, importing video files already stored on your computer, and adding video context from the iLife applications (Mac only).

Downloading Video from the iTunes Store

In Lesson 2, "Working with the iTunes Store," you learned that the iTunes Store offers movies, TV shows, and other video content that you can rent or purchase and then download to your iTunes Library. Like downloading music (which is covered in Lesson 3, "Building Your iTunes Audio Library"), downloading video is a snap because the iTunes Store is integrated into iTunes. Another advantage is that any video you download is in the correct format for not only viewing on your computer, but also on other devices such as iPhones, iPods, and iPads.

The steps you use to download video are similar to those you use to download music. First, browse or search for the video in which you are interested. Second, preview and get information about the video, and download it if it is of interest to you.

One difference between music and video content in the iTunes Store is that you can rent many movies and TV shows instead of purchasing them. Renting is less expensive than purchasing, but also comes with several limitations, as follows:

▶ The rental period for content you rent from the iTunes Store is 30 days. The content remains on your computer or other device for exactly 30 days, which starts as soon as you finish downloading that content to your computer. When the 30-day period ends, the content is deleted from the device automatically. Fortunately, iTunes warns you as the end of the rental period nears, so you won't be completely surprised by disappearing content.

▶ You have 24 hours to finish watching rented content from the time you first play it. You can watch it as often (and much) as you want during that time, but as soon as 24 hours passes after you've hit the Play button, the rented content is deleted from your computer automatically. Note that it doesn't matter how much of the content you've watched; even if it plays for just a few seconds, the viewing period starts and the 24-hour timer kicks in.

▶ You can store rented content only on one device at a time. For example, when you sync rented content onto an iPad, it disappears from your iTunes Library. You can move content between devices as many times as you want, but it can exist on only one device at a time.

Which option you choose depends on whether both options are available to you (some content you can only rent or only purchase) and how sure you are that you want to keep that content permanently. If you are "on the fence" about a movie or TV show and both options are available to you, you can rent it first, and if you decide you want it in your Library permanently, go back to the Store and purchase it. (Unfortunately, the rental cost does not go toward purchasing the content.)

Some movie and TV content is available in the High Definition (HD) format. You usually have the option to purchase or rent the Standard Definition (SD) or the HD version of content, but some content is available in only one version. The version you choose depends on if the devices you use to watch that content support HD, and if they do, whether the quality of that content is worth the additional cost to purchase or rent it.

NOTE: **HD and iPods, iPhones, and iPads**

Apple iPods, iPads, and iPhones can't play all HD content at HD resolutions. The good news is that when you purchase HD content from the iTunes Store, you get the SD version, too. When you sync that content to one of these devices, the appropriate format is used automatically, so you don't need to think about which one to choose.

The general steps to rent or purchase content are the same; you simply click the **Buy** button to purchase content or the **Rent** button to rent it and choose between the SD or HD version (if you have the option). Use the following steps as an example:

1. Use the techniques you learn in Lessons 2 and 3 to find video content of interest to you. You can use the Movies tab to browse for movies, the TV Shows tab to do the same for TV series, or use the Basic or Power Search options to find specific content. When you "drill down" to specific content, you see its information screen as shown in Figure 5.1.

FIGURE 5.1 When you view a movie's or TV show's information screen, you can preview it, see reviews, and download it.

2. To preview video, click the **View Trailer** button or click the **Play** button that appears when you hover over an episode of a TV series. The video begins to play. You can watch the trailer as shown in Figure 5.2 or the 90-second preview, depending on which option you select.

FIGURE 5.2   You can preview video content before you download it, such as watching movie trailers.

3. Scroll around the information screen to see user reviews, critical reviews, related content, and other information that may help you decide if you want to add the content to your Library.

4. If you decide you want to download the content, click the appropriate action button. The options you have depend on the specific content you are considering. In all cases, you see the cost of the option within the action button so you always know how much each option costs. Examples include the following:

   ▶ Buy HD Movie

   ▶ Buy Movie (this is the SD format)

▸ Rent HD Movie

▸ Rent Movie (this is the SD format)

▸ Buy Season (TV shows)

▸ Buy HD Season (series available in HD)

▸ Buy Season Pass

▸ Buy (individual episodes)

▸ Buy All Episodes

▸ Rent (individual episodes)

▸ Buy Video (music videos)

> NOTE: **Season Pass**
> Some currently running shows offer a Season Pass option. When you purchase this option, you get each episode as soon as it is released to the iTunes Store. As you learn in Lesson 2, you can configure iTunes to download these episodes for you automatically so that they appear in your Library immediately after they become available in the iTunes Store.

5. If prompted, enter your iTunes Store password and click **Buy** (or **Rent** if renting content) or just click **Buy** (or **Rent** if renting content). If you allowed iTunes to remember your information for purchasing or renting previously, you won't be prompted and can skip this step.

The content is downloaded to your iTunes Library. You can monitor the progress of the download in the iTunes Information area as shown in Figure 5.3. Downloading video can take a while, but you can continue to use iTunes for other tasks while your content is downloading.

Downloading 2 items
The Sixth Sense / M. Night Shyamalan (3 hours remai...

FIGURE 5.3 The Information area shows you the progress of downloading content from the iTunes Store.

6. You can also monitor the download process by clicking the **Downloads** option in the STORE section of the Source pane, as shown in Figure 5.4. When the download process is complete, iTunes places it into the appropriate category automatically (such as Movies or TV Shows), and the video content is ready for viewing.

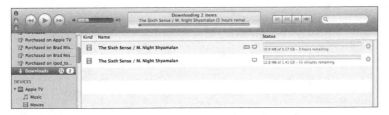

FIGURE 5.4   Here you can see that the HD and SD versions of *The Sixth Sense* are being downloaded.

TIP: **Options**

If you click the downward-facing arrow on the right end of Buy/Rent buttons, you see a menu with various commands, such as gift, which enables you to give the content to someone else, share via Facebook, and so on. One useful option enables you to add content to your wish list, which is much like a shopping cart where you can store content you might be interested in purchasing later. After you add content to your wish list, you can move back to it by clicking the **My Wish List** item on the Quick Links section of the iTunes Store Home page. From your wish list, you can preview or purchase content.

Adding DVD Content to Your Library

You probably have video content on DVD, including movies and TV shows. If you want to be able to store that content on your computer and view it in iTunes or move it onto an iPod, iPhone, or iPad, you can convert the content from the DVD format into a file that you can add to iTunes.

Then, you can watch that content on your computer without the DVD, or more important, move it onto a mobile device.

There are two steps in this process. First, prepare the DVD content for iTunes. Second, add the converted content to iTunes and apply a couple of basic tags.

Preparing DVD Content for iTunes

To convert DVD content into an iTunes-compatible format, you need to use another application because iTunes can't import content from DVDs directly. There are many of these available for both Windows and Macs. A number of them are free. If you don't have one of these, do a web search for "DVD converter" or "DVD ripper" for the type of computer you use. Download and install the application you select on your computer.

> CAUTION: **No Copyright or Use Violations, Please**
>
> Of course, you should use this process only on content you own and that you have the right to use in this manner. As long as you are only converting content on DVDs that you own so that you can view it on your computer or iPhone (your own personal use), you should be okay from a legal perspective. In some cases, content on a DVD may be encoded such that another application can't access it, in which case, this process won't work.

The followings steps show the process with my favorite Mac application for this purpose, Handbrake (http://handbrake.fr/). Other applications require different details, but the general process should be similar:

1. Insert the DVD with the content you want to convert into your computer.

2. Launch the DVD conversion application.

3. Select the DVD as the source you want to convert and choose the specific track you want to have in your iTunes Library. If you convert a disc with multiple tracks, make sure you choose the particular content you want to have on your computer. Everything on the disc is available, including menu effects,

previews, and so on. In most cases, you cannot see the title of the content as it is on the disc. You can usually tell what you want from the track number or length.

4. Select the format into which you want to convert the content. If you want to be able use the converted content on a mobile device, choose a compatible format. For example, most applications offer an iPhone or iPod touch option. Or, if there is an AppleTV option, this format has good quality for viewing on a computer, and is compatible with Apple's mobile devices. You usually want the option with .m4v as the filename extension.

> **NOTE: HD Formats**
>
> If you are converting a DVD in an HD format and want to be able to watch the HD version on your computer and view it on a mobile device, you might have to convert it twice: once in an HD format and once in a format compatible with your mobile device. In the second part of this process, you should give each version unique names so that you know which is which.

5. Configure other options if you want to. In most cases, you can just use one of the default options.

6. Name and choose a location in which to save the converted content. See Figure 5.5 for an example showing the conversion of an episode of *Star Trek Deep Space Nine* into the AppleTV format.

7. Start the conversion process. The amount of time the process takes depends on your computer's processing power, the efficiency of the application, the conversion settings you use, amount of content, and so on. After you've converted a few items, you'll get a feel for how long the process takes with your setup. When the process is done, you're ready to add the converted content to iTunes.

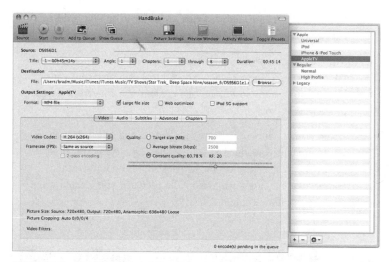

FIGURE 5.5 This episode of *Star Trek Deep Space Nine* is being converted using the AppleTV format.

TIP: **Queue It Up!**

Some DVD conversion applications offer a Queue option so that you can select and configure the conversion of multiple items on the same disc. This is perfect for converting a disc with episodes of a TV show on it. Start the first episode as described in these steps. While the process is ongoing, use steps 3 (of course, you can't change discs) through 6 to configure the next item to convert. Add that item to the queue. Repeat these steps until you've selected all the content on the disc. The application converts each item you select in the same order you selected them. So, you can go about your business while the disc is being converted.

Importing Converted DVD Content into iTunes

After the DVD content has been converted, add it to your iTunes Library and add some basic tags to it, as follows:

1. Choose **File, Add File to Library** (Windows) or **File, Add to Library** (Mac).

2. Move to and select the converted content, and then click **Open** (Windows) or **Choose** (Mac). The content is copied into your iTunes Library. In most cases, any content you convert is stored in the Movies source.

3. Using iTunes' browse or search tools, find and select the converted content you added to your iTunes Library, as shown in Figure 5.6. You can select the Movies source and browse the converted content or search using the filename you created when you converted the content.

FIGURE 5.6   Here I've selected converted content because I'm going to add some basic tags to it.

4. Choose **File, Get Info**.

5. Click the **Info** tab, as shown in Figure 5.7.

6. Enter as much information about the content as you want to have; the minimum information is the name of the content. If the content is from a TV show, you should enter episode number as the track number. You should also choose a genre.

7. Click the **Video** tab, as shown in Figure 5.8

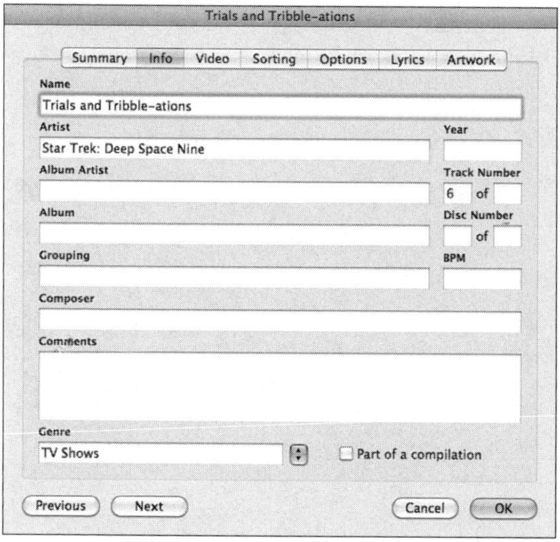

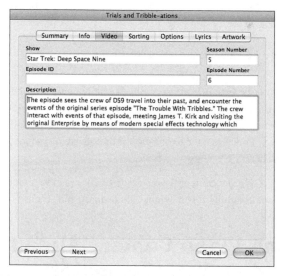

FIGURE 5.7   Use the Info tab to rename the converted content and set the genre.

FIGURE 5.8   Use the Video tab to enter additional information about the content, such as a description of its plot.

8. Enter the applicable information about the content, such as the title of the series, season number, episode number, description, and so on.

9. Click the **Options** tab, as shown in Figure 5.9.

FIGURE 5.9   Use the Options tab to choose the Media Kind for the imported content.

10. Choose the type of content on the Media Kind menu. This is an important setting because it determines the category on the Source list in which the content will be stored (Movies, TV Shows, Podcasts, and so on). For most converted content, you will choose **TV Show** or **Movie**.

11. Click **OK**. The content is now ready to view, add to a mobile device (assuming it is a compatible format), and so on.

Adding Video Content Already Stored on Your Computer

iTunes supports the playback of a number of types of video files, including MP4, MV4, MOV, and most other common video file formats. Generally, any file format compatible with QuickTime can be viewed in iTunes. There are other supported formats, as well. If you download files in a supported format or convert them into a format iTunes can manage, it's easy to add the files to your iTunes Library, where you can watch them, add them to a mobile device, and so on.

The steps you use to add video files already stored on your computer to iTunes are the same as when you add video files you've converted from a DVD to iTunes. See the section "Importing Converted DVD Content into iTunes," earlier in this lesson, for the details.

Adding Video Content from an iLife Application on a Mac

The iLife applications iMovie and GarageBand are integrated with iTunes, so its easy to move content from one of these applications to your iTunes Library. The most likely application you use for this purpose is iMovie. However, you can move music you create in GarageBand to your iTunes Library just as easily.

The steps to move a movie you created in iMovie to your iTunes Library are as follows:

1. In iMovie, Ctrl-click or right-click the project you want to add to your iTunes Library.

2. Choose **iTunes** from the pop-up menu, as shown in Figure 5.10. The Publish to iTunes sheet appears, as shown in Figure 5.11.

3. Select the sizes you want to be available in iTunes by checking their check boxes. You can use the devices shown at the top of the sheet as a guide. For example, if you are going to watch the movie on your computer and on an iPhone, check **Mobile** and **Large**.

4. Click **Publish**. iMovie prepares the movie and sends it to the Movies folder in your iTunes library. Once it's there, you can do all the tasks with it that you can do with video from other sources.

FIGURE 5.10   It's easy to move an iMovie project into iTunes.

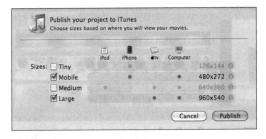

FIGURE 5.11   You can choose the size for the movie in iTunes depending on where you are going to use it.

Summary

In this lesson, you learned how to stock your iTunes Library with video content from the iTunes Store, DVDs, files already stored on your computer, and iLife applications. In the next lesson, you learn how to use iTunes to enjoy your video.

LESSON 6

Watching Video

In this lesson, you learn how to configure iTunes to play back movies, TV shows, and other video. You also learn how to find video to watch. Lastly, you learn a number of ways you can use iTunes to watch video.

Setting Video-Viewing Options

As you learn throughout this lesson, iTunes offers a number of ways to watch video content. Your preferred method is determined through a few preference settings. Open the Preferences dialog box (**Edit**, **Preferences** on a Windows PC or **iTunes**, **Preferences** on a Mac).

On the Playback tab, you have the options shown in the Figure 6.1 and listed here:

▶ **Play Movies and TV Shows.** You have a number of options to determine where video plays by default; you can choose other ways to watch regardless of the setting on this menu. Select **in the artwork viewer** to display movies and TV shows in the Item Artwork/Video Viewer pane at the bottom of the Source pane. Pick **in the iTunes window** to display video content in the Content pane of the iTunes window. Choose **in a separate window** to have iTunes open a new window to display movies and TV shows. Select **full screen** to have movies and TV shows play with the video content filling the screen and the rest of the interface hidden. The **full screen (with visuals)** option is similar, but if you play a playlist with both video and audio-only content, when the audio-only content plays, the Visualizer appears on the screen.

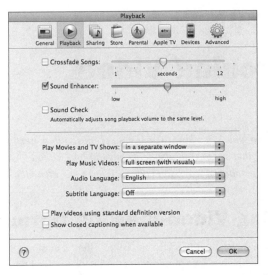

FIGURE 6.1   Use the preference settings toward the lower part of the Playback pane to configure how video content plays.

▶ **Play Music Videos.** The menu offers the same options as the previous one except it determines what happens when you play music videos as opposed to movies and TV shows.

▶ **Audio Language.** Choose your default language on this menu. When video content has multiple audio tracks, your preferred language is played by default.

▶ **Subtitle Language.** Use this menu to choose the language in which subtitles are displayed.

▶ **Play videos using standard definition version.** If your Library contains both High Definition (HD) and Standard Definition (SD) versions of video content (such as HD movies you download from the iTunes Store), this option causes the SD version to play. If unchecked, the HD version plays.

▶ **Show closed captioning when available.** When this enabled, if video content includes close captioning, you see it on the screen.

There's an additional setting on the Advanced pane, as shown in Figure 6.2. If you play video in a separate window, you can check the **Keep movie window on top of all other windows** to ensure your video is never hidden by other open windows on your computer.

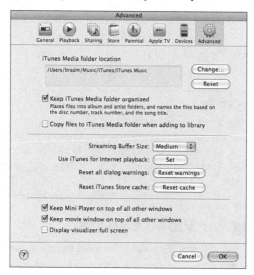

FIGURE 6.2   Use the Keep movie window on top of all other windows check box to ensure video playing in a separate window doesn't get covered over by other windows.

> TIP: **More on Video Preferences**
>
> If you choose the In Artwork Viewer preference, you can open a separate window to watch video by clicking the Video Viewer pane. If you choose In the iTunes Window option, you can display video in full screen with a single mouse click. Either of these settings actually gives you two viewing options, so I recommend you pick one of these two. In most cases, in the iTunes window is a good choice.

Browsing and Searching for Video Content

In Lesson 4, "Listening to Music," you learned the details of browsing and searching for music. The good news is that the same skills you learned in that lesson apply to this because iTunes uses the same browsing and searching capabilities for video content as it does for music. There are some minor variations, however, because you are working with video content, but the basic approach is the same.

Video content is stored in four sources under LIBRARY in the Source pane: Music (music videos), Movies, TV Shows, and Podcasts (video podcasts, which you learn about in Lesson 9, "Subscribing to and Enjoying Podcasts").

> **NOTE: Overview Only**
> Because of the similarity to browsing and searching for music, the details are not repeated here. If you haven't read through Lesson 4 yet, do so now so that you understand how browsing and searching works in detail. Then come back here to see how your skills apply to video content.

Browsing for Video Content

To browse for video, select the source you want to browse and choose the view in which you want to browse that source. The view options are the same as for music: List, Album List, Grid, and Cover Flow. (See Figure 6.3 for an example of browsing movies with the Cover Flow view.) Lists for video content work the same as for music, too. You can sort the lists by clicking a column heading, move columns around, and so on. You can also use the View Options dialog box to configure the columns that appear when you browse video sources using a view with lists (all but the Grid view).

You can use the Browser with the List and Album List views. This also works like it does for music, and you can configure the options using the View menu. You can choose to show different columns when viewing movies versus TV shows. When browsing the Movies source, the columns that are most useful are Genre and Artist; whereas when you browse the TV Shows source, the useful columns are Genres, Shows, and Seasons.

FIGURE 6.3   The Cover Flow view displays the artwork associated with video or a frame of the video if it doesn't have artwork.

TIP: **TV Shows in Grid View**

If you browse the TV Shows source in Grid view with the TV Shows option, you can click a grid to watch that show. If there are multiple episodes for that show, the episode you were most recently watching plays or the next unwatched episode plays if you finished the last episode you watched.

Searching for Video Content

You can also search for video content using the Search tool in the upper-right corner of the iTunes window. At the risk of repetition, searching for video content works just like searching for music does. When you search the TV Shows source, you can search by All, Show, or Title. When you search the Movies source, you can search by All or Title.

To search, select the source you want to search, choose the attribute by which you want to search (if you don't make a choice, you search by All), and enter a search term in the Search tool. As you type, iTunes identifies content that matches your search and presents it in the Content pane.

Watching Movies, TV Shows, and Music Videos

Watching video content follows the standard iTunes pattern. First, browse or search for the content you want to watch. Second, select and play the content. What happens next depends on the video-viewing preference you set earlier in this lesson. Following are examples of each preference.

Watching Video in the iTunes Window

In this mode, the video content fills the entire space where the Source and Content panes usually appear. At the top and bottom of the iTunes window, you see information and controls you can use to control the video playback. You can also use onscreen controls that appear.

Here's how it works. Select the content you want to watch. Click the **Play** button or double-click the content. The video starts to play as shown in Figure 6.4.

You can control the video using the tools on the iTunes toolbar at the top of the window or the onscreen video toolbar that appears at the bottom of the window, as shown in Figure 6.5.

The controls available to you (shown in both Figure 6.4 and 6.5) are as follows:

> ▶ **Exit.** Click this to exit the video and return to the iTunes window showing the Source and Content panes.

> ▶ **Rewind/Previous.** Click and hold to rewind. Click to move to and play the previous video in the current source.

> ▶ **Play/Pause.** Starts the video if it isn't playing; pauses it if it is playing.

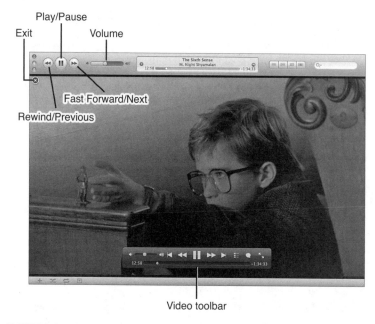

FIGURE 6.4   Here, I'm watching *The Sixth Sense* within the iTunes window.

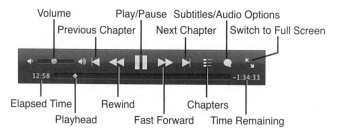

FIGURE 6.5   The onscreen video toolbar gives you a lot of control over video.

> ► **Fast Forward/Next.** Click and hold to fast-forward. Click once to move to the next video in the current source.

> ► **Volume.** Drag to the left to lower the volume or to the right to increase it.

▶ **Previous Chapter.** Move to the previous chapter in the current video.

▶ **Rewind.** Click and hold to rewind in the current video.

▶ **Fast Forward.** Click and hold to fast-forward in the current video.

▶ **Chapters.** Click to see a list of chapters in the current video; click a chapter to jump to it. This appears only when the video content has chapters.

▶ **Subtitles/Audio Options.** Click and hold to see and choose the audio options for the current video, such as language options or surround sound. Configure subtitles for the current video if they are available.

▶ **Switch to Full Screen.** Click this to view the video in Full Screen mode; more detail about this is provided later in this lesson.

You can use the Timeline bar in the Information area at the top of the iTunes window and on the video toolbar to get information about the video, including elapsed and remaining times. You can also drag the Playhead to the left or move backward in the video or to the right to move forward in the video.

> TIP: **Changing Info**
>
> In the Information area at the top of the window, if you click the **Artist** line (under the Title line), the display changes to be the name of the current chapter. If you click the **Time Remaining**, it changes to be the total time of the video.

If you stop moving the mouse or don't make any other inputs for a few seconds, the onscreen controls disappear. To make them reappear, move the mouse. The controls at the top of the iTunes window are always available to you.

When you're done watching the video, click the **Exit** button. The video stops playing and you return to the iTunes window, which is showing the Source pane and Content pane.

> **NOTE: Tracking What You've Watched**
>
> Video content you haven't watched is marked with a blue dot on lists in the Content pane. As you watch a movie or episode of a TV series, its dot gets emptier until, finally, it disappears when you've watched all of a specific video, such as a movie or an episode of a TV series.

Watching Video in a Separate Window

You can also watch video in a separate window that is independent of the iTunes window.

To do this, select the content you want to watch. Click the **Play** button or double-click the content. A new window appears, and the video starts to play, as shown in Figure 6.6.

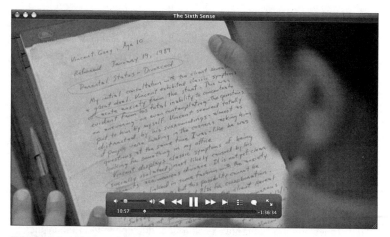

FIGURE 6.6   You can watch video in a separate window, as you see here.

The name of the window is the name of the video you are playing. You can move and resize the window as you can other windows you work with.

When you move the pointer over the video window, the onscreen tools appear. These are the same as for video playing in the iTunes window. (See the previous section for the details about these controls.) If you don't move within the window for a few seconds, the tools disappear.

To stop the video, click the window's **Close** button. The video stops, and
the window closes.

> NOTE: **Rented Content**
>
> The first time you watch rented content from the iTunes Store, a
> prompt appears informing you that the viewing period for the con-
> tent is starting. If you confirm this, the prompt goes away, the video
> plays, and the 24-hour viewing period starts. You can watch the
> content as much as you want over the next 24 hours, but at that
> point, the rented content is deleted from your Library. When you
> see rented content in lists, you see how much time remains in the
> 24-hour playing period (if you've watched the video) or in the 30-day
> rental period (if you haven't watched it).

Watching Video in Full Screen

When you watch video in Full Screen mode, the iTunes interface disappears, and the video content takes over the entire screen. Like the other
methods, first select the video you want play, and then click the **Play**
button, double-click the content, or press the spacebar. iTunes' windows
and panes disappear, and the video starts playing and fills the screen, as
shown in Figure 6.7.

The onscreen controls work in the same way as when you watch video
within the iTunes window. To exit, click the **Exit** button or click the
Reduce button that appears at the far right of the video toolbar. If you
started with the Full Screen mode, the video appears in a separate window;
close that window to stop the video. If you started with the video playing
in the iTunes window, you move back to the video playing in the iTunes
window.

Watching Video in the Video Viewer

If you choose the Video Viewer mode, video you play appears in the Item
Artwork/Video Viewer pane located at the bottom of the Source pane, as
shown in Figure 6.8. Video is quite small in this pane, even if you have the
iTunes window at a very large size. You control the video with the controls
at the top of the iTunes window. If you click the video, it opens and plays
in a separate window.

FIGURE 6.7 In Full Screen mode, the video fills your computer screen.

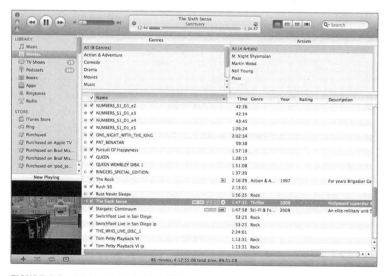

FIGURE 6.8 Video in the Video Viewer pane is quite small, but it can be useful to preview content so that you can see both the video and its information in the Content pane at the same time.

NOTE: **Back Where You Left Off**

By default, video content is set to resume playing where you last stopped playing it. So, if you watch part of a movie and then stop playing it, the next time you start it, it picks up where you left off. There is actually an option you can set for each item in your Library that controls this; you learn about this in Lesson 7, "Tagging iTunes Content."

Summary

In this lesson, you learned how to enjoy the video content in your iTunes Library. You learned to set video preferences, where to look for video content, and how to watch video using a variety of iTunes video tools. In the next lesson, you learn how to tag the content in your iTunes Library.

LESSON 7

Tagging iTunes Content

In this lesson, you learn the importance of tagging content in your Library to make it easier to find, browse, include in playlists, and so on. You also learn how to work with iTunes automatic tagging and how to tag content manually for individual items and for groups of items.

Understanding Tagging

If you've read through the previous lessons, you already have a good idea of what tagging is all about, which is to add information to your iTunes content. This information keeps your content organized and helps you find it through browsing and searching. For example, when you use the Browser to browse for music or video, the categories by which you browse are tags on the content you are browsing. And, you also learned how to configure and use the columns in lists; each column is a tag.

You can also use tags to perform tasks with content, such as creating playlists (which is covered in Lesson 8, "Creating and Using Playlists").

Some tags, called options, impact how your content works. For example, you can configure content to start or stop at certain points, remember where you left off playing it, and so on.

iTunes automatically tags some kinds of content for you, such as music or video that you download from the iTunes Store or audio CDs when you import them to your Library.

You can also manually tag your content to add more information or in those cases where iTunes doesn't tag content for you automatically.

Although tagging might not seem like the most fun you can have with iTunes, it is an important topic because keeping your content properly tagged makes working with it much easier and faster.

Working with Automatic Tagging

iTunes applies a number of tags to all content automatically, regardless of how that content gets into your Library. Some of the more important of these tags are as follows:

▶ **Kind** identifies the type of content, such as AAC audio or MPEG-4 video file.

▶ **Time** shows how long the content plays.

▶ **Last Played** shows you when you last listened to or watched the content.

▶ **Plays** is the number of times you have played content.

▶ **Size** indicates the size of the content's file stored on your computer.

▶ **Where** shows where the content's file is stored on your computer.

You can't change these tags within iTunes, but they provide very useful information for you, especially for creating playlists.

When you add content to your iTunes Library from the iTunes Store, a number of tags come with that content. These include identification information (name, artist, album, year, genre, and so on), options, artwork, and several technical tags about that content. You can change many of the tags for downloaded content after you've added it to your Library if you choose to.

When you add content by importing audio CDs, iTunes can tag that content for you automatically. It can also add album artwork for you. Make sure you've configured iTunes to automatically tag content you import from CDs with the following settings available on the iTunes Preferences dialog box:

▶ **Automatically retrieve CD track names from the Internet.** Located on the General tab, this setting causes iTunes to connect to the Internet and attempt to identify audio CDs when you insert them into your computer. If a CD is found in the online databases, iTunes adds its tags (CD name, artist, and track names) to the CD. When you browse or play the CD, you can see this information. More important, when you import a CD, this information is added to the imported content automatically. (Importing audio CDs is covered in Lesson 3, "Building Your iTunes Audio Library.")

▶ **Automatically download missing album artwork.** This setting, located on the Store tab, causes iTunes to try to download artwork from the iTunes Store and apply it to any content in your Library that is missing artwork. (Any content you purchase from the iTunes Store already has artwork associated with it.) The caveat here is that the content missing artwork must be available in the iTunes Store; so if you've added content that is not available in the Store, you have to add artwork manually.

Tagging Content with the Get Info Command

To see all the tags available for content in your Library, select that content by clicking a song, movie, TV episode, or any other content in the Content pane. Then, choose **File**, **Get Info** or press Ctl+I (Windows) or Cmd+I (Mac). The resulting window has seven tabs, with each tab providing a category of information about the selected content.

At the bottom of the dialog box, you see the following buttons:

▶ **Previous.** Click this to show the tags for the previous item in the source in which you selected the current item. This makes it easy to work with tags for a series of items.

▶ **Next.** This button takes you to the next item in the current source.

▶ **Cancel.** This closes the dialog box without saving any changes you make.

▶ **OK.** This button closes the dialog box and saves any changes you made.

The general process to change tags is to open the dialog box, work with one or more of the tabs to view or change information, click **Next** or **Previous** to work with other content, and then click **OK** when you've finished.

The following subsections show how you can use each tab.

Working with the Summary Tab

The Summary tab presents a variety of tags to you, as shown in Figure 7.1. Unlike the other tabs, you can't change any of the tags on the Summary tab. However, it provides useful information for you about the content, including many of the tags that iTunes applies automatically for all the content in your Library.

FIGURE 7.1 Although you can't change the information on the Summary tab, it can still be very useful to you.

Working with the Info Tab

The Info tab provides a number of informational tags about the content, as shown in Figure 7.2. You can use the Info tab to view or change any of the tags you see.

FIGURE 7.2   The Info tab contains important identification information for your content.

Most of the tags are self-explanatory, such as Name, Artist, Year, and so on. You can view these tags if the relevant fields have information in them or you can add information to any empty tags. You can also change existing tags by editing or typing over their contents.

Some of the tags that benefit from a little explanation are the following:

▶ **Album Artist.** You can use this tag to associate content with an artist that might be different from that shown in the Artist field. For example, you might have music from the same person, with some from the person as a solo artist and some as a member of a group. You can apply the same Album Artist tag to both types of music. Then, you group or sort by Album Artist so that all the music associated with that person appears together. If you sort or group by Artist instead, that music appears as separate entries on lists based on the person's name and the group's name.

▶ **Grouping.** This is a general tag you can apply to a group of music that you want to be able to list together without changing the tags that are important to the individual items. This tag is available in the View Options dialog box, and you can add it to lists to be able to sort by the Grouping.

▶ **Beats per Minute (BPM).** This is a measure of the tempo of the music. You can add it or change it in the BPM field. You can use BPM as you can other tags, such as to create a playlist or sort the Content pane.

▶ **Genre.** Genre can be used for browsing and also to create playlists. Choose the genre for the content on the Genre menu. If a genre by which you want to classify content isn't listed on the menu, you can add it by selecting **Custom** at the top of the menu and then typing the genre you want to add. That genre is added to the menu and associated with the current content. You can use the custom genres you create just like the default genres.

▶ **Part of a compilation.** This check box indicates the item is from a compilation album, meaning one that includes music from other artists or even from multiple albums (originally). Greatest hits albums are compilations, as are any other album that contains songs not released on the same album. When this check box is checked, the content is designated as being from one of these albums. When you group or sort showing compilations together, the contents appear together. When you don't group compilations together, the individual tracks can be scattered throughout the Content pane based on other tags (such as Artist).

Working with the Video Tab

This straightforward tab, shown in Figure 7.3, contains identification information for video content, such as movies and TV shows.

To keep episodes of a TV series organized (such as when you import them after converting them from a DVD), make sure you enter the series title in the Show field and the season and episode numbers in their respective fields. This keeps the episodes grouped and organized according to the order they occur in the series.

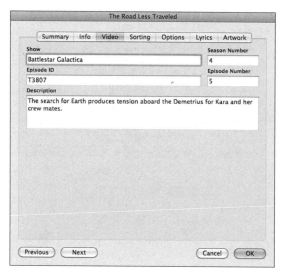

FIGURE 7.3   The Video tab contains important information applicable to video content.

The Description tag is a good place to store a plot summary or other information about the video content. You can view this on lists in the Content pane, which makes selection of specific content easier.

Working with the Sorting Tab

This tab enables you to apply "sorting" tags to content. These tags are used when you sort lists in the Content pane, but don't change the fundamental tags for your content. There are two columns of tags on the pane. The column on the left lists the "real" tags for the content. The content on the right lists the "sorting" tags. The example in Figure 7.4 might make the concept clearer. This shows the Sorting pane for music from Jon Foreman, who also happens to be the lead singer for the group Switchfoot. By applying the Sort Artist tag of Switchfoot, when I sort a list by Artist, this music is grouped with music by Switchfoot rather than by Jon Foreman. However, the actual artist is still set to be Jon Foreman. Sorting tags simply enable you to have more control over how your content sorts without changing the primary tags for your content.

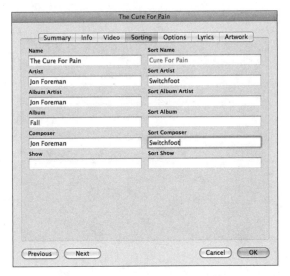

FIGURE 7.4 The Sorting tab enables you to apply tags that are used for sorting while maintaining the content's original tags.

Working with the Options Tab

The Options tab, see Figure 7.5, enables you to configure how content plays, how it is classified, and how you rate it. The options you can adjust include the following:

> ▶ **Volume Adjustment.** You can change content's relative volume so that it is either louder or quieter than "normal." This is useful when specific content has a default volume level that is too high or too low. When you set the slider to the right, you increase the relative volume of the content; when you set it to the left, the content plays quieter.

> ▶ **Equalizer Preset.** You can use the iTunes Equalizer to configure the relative volume of sound frequencies. Choosing an Equalizer preset saves specific Equalizer settings with the content so that they are used automatically whenever you play that content.

> ▶ **Media Kind.** This is an important setting because it determines which source in the Source pane stores the content. The options

are Music, Audiobook, Voice Memo, Music Video, Movie, TV Show, Podcast, and iTunes U. The options on the menu are determined by the type of file you've selected. For example, if you select a movie, you won't see the Music option. When you make a selection on this menu, the content is stored in the related category in the Source pane. So, if you import a TV show from DVD into your Library, you set the media kind to TV Show so that it is stored in the TV Shows source.

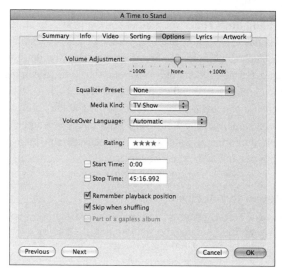

FIGURE 7.5   The Options tab enables you to change how content plays.

▶ **VoiceOver Language (Mac Only).** Choose the language that is used when VoiceOver is enabled and you point to items in your iTunes Library.

NOTE: **VoiceOver**

The Mac's VoiceOver feature causes the computer to read text elements on the screen out loud when that text is selected. Though designed primarily for sight-impaired people, it works for anyone who wants to hear what they have selected.

▶ **Rating.** You can give content a rating from one to five stars. You can use ratings in various ways, such as to create criteria for playlists (such as include only my five-star songs) or to sort lists in the Content pane. To rate the content, click the dot representing the number of stars you want to give the content. For example, to give a song three stars, click the center (third) dot. Stars appear up to the point at which you click. In other words, before you click, you see dots. After you click a dot, you see stars representing your rating (such as three stars).

▶ **Start and Stop Time.** You can set content to start or stop at certain points. This can be useful if you don't want to hear all of a track, such as when a song has an introduction you don't want to hear each time the song plays. To set a start time, check the **Start Time** check box and enter a time in the format minutes:seconds. When you play the content, it starts playing at the time you enter. To set a stop time, check the **Stop Time** check box and enter a time in the format minutes:seconds. When you play the content, it stops playing at the time you enter.

NOTE: **Return to Full Playing Time**

When you set a start or stop time, you don't change the content's file in any way. You can play the whole content again by unchecking the **Start Time** or **Stop Time** check boxes.

▶ **Remember playback position.** This check box causes iTunes to "remember" where leave off playing content. The next time you play that content, it starts where you left off instead of at the beginning; if unchecked, the content always starts over. This is useful for movies, TV shows, podcasts, and so on that you usually listen to or view all the way through. The playback position is remembered even if you quit iTunes and come back to it later.

▶ **Skip when shuffling.** When you play content in Shuffle mode, iTunes randomly selects the order the content plays in. When this box is checked, the content is skipped when use Shuffle mode to play the source it is in. For example, if you have chapters of an

audiobook in the same source as some music, you probably don't
want to mix the chapters in with your songs.

▶ **Part of a gapless album.** When iTunes plays songs, it inserts a
gap of silence between the songs, just as you would "hear" when
playing a CD or album. This gap can disrupt certain kinds of
content, such as a live recording where you should hear applause
between the tracks rather than silence. When this check box is
checked, iTunes doesn't add a gap between the tracks; instead,
they play continuously one to the next.

> NOTE: **Inactive Options**
>
> Some options don't apply to the selected content and so are dis-
> abled on the Options tab. For example, you can't tag an episode of
> a TV show as being part of a gapless album.

Working with the Lyrics Tab

You can store lyrics (or other text for that matter) on the Lyrics tab.
Unfortunately, the viewing options for lyrics within iTunes are limited. To
view lyrics, you must open the Lyrics tab, which isn't convenient because
you can't use iTunes' controls when the Lyrics pane is displayed. (When
the Get Info dialog box is open, it always remains on top of iTunes.)
However, lyrics are very useful when you move music onto an iPod, iPad,
or iPhone because you see them on the Now Playing screen.

To add lyrics to a song, type them in the Lyrics pane or copy and paste
them there.

> TIP: **Finding Lyrics**
>
> A quick web search for just about any song title followed by the
> word "lyrics" takes you to a web page with the lyrics for the song.
> Copy the lyrics from the page and paste into the Lyrics pane.

Working with the Artwork Tab

As discussed in the earlier lessons, artwork such as album covers or other
images or graphics can be associated with your content. You can also associate multiple images for the same piece of content. You use the Artwork

tab to manually configure the art associated with any content, as shown in Figure 7.6.

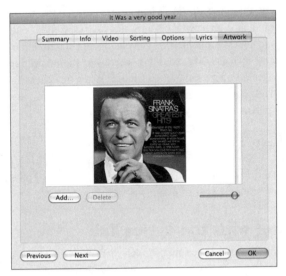

FIGURE 7.6   You can use the Artwork tab to view, change, or add images or other graphics to your content.

To add and configure artwork for content, complete the following steps:

1. Prepare the artwork you are going to associate with the content. You can use graphics in the usual formats, such as JPG, TIFF, GIF, and so on.

2. Open the **Artwork** tab for the content you want to associate the art with. If artwork currently exists, you see it in the pane.

> TIP: **Album Art**
>
> Great sources of artwork for your CDs are online CD retailers (such as Amazon.com). Most of these provide the album cover as an image when you view a CD. You can download these images to your computer and then add them to songs in your Library.

3. Click **Add**. The Choose dialog box appears.

4. Move to and select the image you want use.

5. Click **Open** (Windows) or **Choose** (Mac). The image is added to the Artwork pane.

6. Use the slider under the image box to change the size of the previews you see in the window. Drag the slider to the right to make the image larger or to the left to make it smaller. This doesn't change the image; instead, it impacts just the size of the image as you currently see it in the Info window. This is especially useful when you associate lots of images with a song because you can see them all at the same time.

7. Repeat steps 3 through 6 to continue adding images to the Artwork tab until you have added all the images you want. The default image for the content is the one on the left of the image box.

8. To change the order of the images, drag them in the image box.

If content has more than one piece of artwork associated with it, click the arrows that appear at the top of the Item Artwork/Video Viewer pane to see each piece of art.

TIP: **Video Art**

By default, video content uses a poster frame as its image rather than the content of the Artwork tab. You can set the poster frame for any video content by playing that content and moving the Playhead to the frame you want to use. Right-click the video and choose **Set Poster Frame** on the menu that appears. The frame that is displayed when you choose the command becomes the poster frame for the video.

Tagging Multiple Items at the Same Time

You will sometimes want to apply the same tags to multiple items. For example, you might want to change the genre for or add the same artwork to all the songs on an album. You can use the Next and Previous buttons to move to each item, but there is a much faster way.

Select multiple items in the Content pane by holding the Ctrl (Windows) or Cmd (Mac) key as you click each item. If the items are next to each other, you can hold the Shift down while you click the first item you want to choose, and then click the last item you want to include; those two items are selected along with all of the items between them. Choose **File**, **Get Info**. The Multiple Item Information dialog box appears, as shown in Figure 7.7.

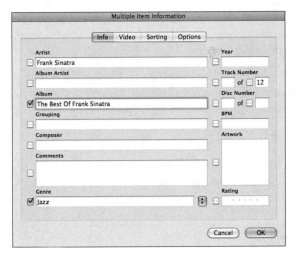

FIGURE 7.7   Using the Multiple Item Information dialog box is an efficient way to apply tags to multiple items at the same time.

Use the tabs, fields, and other tools on the dialog box to apply tabs to all the selected items. These work much like when you are tagging an individual item. When you input to any of the fields, menus, or other controls, their check boxes are checked to indicate that the tag is going to be applied to all the items you selected. You won't see all the tabs or tags available for the dialog box when you are working with a single item, but most of them are there. (The Summary and Lyrics tabs don't appear because those make sense for only a single item at a time.)

> CAUTION: **Artwork and Multiple Items**
>
> You don't see any artwork for the selected items in the Artwork box even if they all have the same image. This can be misleading because you can't tell whether the selected items have images already.

> TIP: **Dragging Art**
>
> You can drag an image into the Artwork box to replace the art-work for all the items with the new image.

Tagging Content in the Content Pane

You can also edit some tags directly in the Content pane:

- ▶ To edit a text tag, click once on the tag you want to change. (If you double-click instead, the content plays. After a moment, the tag is highlighted to indicate you can change it. Edit the text and press Enter (Windows) or Return (Mac) to save the new tag.

- ▶ To rate an item, click the content you want to rate and move to the Rating column. Click the dot for the number of stars you want to apply. The appropriate number of dots become stars.

- ▶ You can also rate an item by right-clicking it. On the resulting menu, choose **Rating** and then choose the number of stars.

- ▶ To get album art, right-click an item and choose **Get Album Artwork**.

Summary

In this lesson, you learned why tagging content is important and how iTunes tags content for you automatically. You also learned how to tag content manually, both individually and in groups. In the next lesson, you learn how to create, manage, and use playlists.

LESSON 8

Creating and Using Playlists

In this lesson, you learn about one of iTunes most useful features: playlists. Playlists enable you to customize your iTunes experience as much as you want. And, you usually create a playlist as part of other tasks, such as moving content onto an iPhone, iPod, or iPad. In addition, iTunes creates several playlists for you that are quite useful and fun.

Understanding Playlists

Simply put, playlists are collections of content in your Library that you create, that iTunes creates for you based on criteria you define, or that iTunes creates mostly on its own. The three types of playlists you learn about in this lesson are as follows:

▶ **Standard.** A standard playlist (which I just call a playlist from here on) is a set of content you define manually. You put the specific songs or videos you want in a playlist and do what you will with them. You can include the same song multiple times, mix and match songs from many CDs, put songs in any order you choose, and basically control every aspect of that content collection.

▶ **Smart.** A smart playlist is *smart* because you don't put content in it manually. Instead, you tell iTunes which kind of content you want included by the attributes of that content, such as genre or artist, and iTunes picks the playlist's content for you automatically. For example, you can create a music playlist based on a specific genre, such as jazz, that you have listened to in the past few days. You can also configure various properties of a smart playlist, such as how much content it contains. The really cool thing is that smart playlists can be dynamic, meaning the content they contain is updated over time based on criteria you define. As you add, listen to, or change content in your Library, the contents of a smart playlist can change to reflect what you've done.

▶ **iTunes-created.** There are several playlists that iTunes creates for you. The purchased playlists automatically contain the content you've downloaded from the iTunes Store; there's a purchased playlist for each device on which you downloaded content. The iTunes Genius creates playlists that are "like" songs you choose, and it creates mixes for you. There's also the iTunes DJ that creates playlists for you on-the-fly; if you have a network, other people can request songs for the iTunes DJ to play.

The last thing to understand about playlists is that they don't actually contain content; they only contain pointers to content in your Library. This means a track can appear in multiple playlists at the same time, but there is only one actual file for that content. This means you can add or delete items to a playlist without changing the content in your Library.

There are many ways to use playlists: you can listen to or watch them, put them on discs, move them to an mobile device, share them over a network, and much more. Over time, you might find that playlists are one of the most useful and fun features iTunes offers.

Because they are so useful, you are likely to create and use a lot of playlists. Fortunately, you can use folders to keep your playlists organized in the Source pane; all the playlists you create are stored in the appropriately named PLAYLISTS section of the Source pane. (iTunes-created playlists appear in other places.)

NOTE: Different Icons for Different Kinds of Playlists

In the Source pane, the playlist icon is a musical note with lines connected to it. A smart playlist has the gear icon. Genius playlists have the "nuclear" icon, and the Genius mixes source has four small boxes. The iTunes DJ's icon is a stack of discs. Folders containing playlists have the folder icon.

Creating and Managing Playlists

Playlists are great for collecting content you want to listen to or watch on demand; think of playlists as your own greatest hits collections. They are useful for moving content onto iPods, iPhones, and iPads because you can collect content to match the amount of storage space you want to consume on these devices. You can also use playlists to burn CDs, and you can share playlists with others over a local network.

With a playlist, you can determine exactly which content is included and the order in which that content plays. You can use playlists to collect any type of content, including music, movies, TV shows, and so on. Although you generally include only one type of content, such as music, in a single playlist, you can also mix and match content types. For example, you might want to include a group's music videos in a playlist that also contains its music. Playlists are easy to create, and they never change over time—unless you intentionally change them.

Creating a Playlist

You can create a playlist in two ways. You can create a playlist that is empty (meaning it doesn't include any content), or you can choose content and then create a playlist that includes the content you chose.

The place you start depends on what you have in mind. If you want to create a collection of content but aren't sure which specific content you want to start with, create an empty playlist. If you know of at least some of the content you intend to include, choose that content and create the playlist.

You can create an empty playlist by using any of the following techniques:

- ▶ Choose **File, New Playlist**.

- ▶ Press **Ctrl+N** (Windows) or **Cmd+N** (Mac).

- ▶ Click the **Create Playlist** button, which is the plus sign (+) in the lower-left corner of the iTunes window.

Whichever method you use results in an empty playlist in the Source pane; its name is highlighted to show you that it is ready for you to edit. Type a name for the playlist and press **Enter** (Windows) or **Return** (Mac)—you can name a playlist anything you want. The playlist is renamed and selected in the Source pane. Because the playlist is currently empty, the Content pane is empty when the playlist is selected. The playlist is ready for you to add content; you learn how to do so later in this lesson.

> NOTE: **Order, Order**
>
> iTunes lists playlists in the PLAYLISTS section in the following order (top to bottom of the window): iTunes DJ, folders of playlists and smart playlists, smart playlists not in a folder, and playlists not in a folder. Within folders, playlists appear in alphabetic order, as do the smart playlists not in a folder and the playlists not in a folder. So, when you name or rename a playlist, it jumps to the location on the Source list where it belongs based on this order.

If you already know some content you want to place in a playlist, you can create the playlist so that it includes that content as soon as you create it. Browse or search the Library to find the content you want to include in the playlist. For example, you can browse for all the songs in a specific genre or search for music by a specific artist. In the Content pane, select the content you want to place in the playlist.

> TIP: **Selecting Tracks**
>
> Remember that you can select tracks that are next to one another by holding down the Shift key while you click them. You can choose multiple tracks that aren't next to one another by holding down the Ctrl key (Windows) or the Cmd key (Mac) while you click them.

Choose **File, New Playlist from Selection** or press **Ctrl+Shift+N** (Windows) or **Cmd+Shift+N** (Mac). A new playlist appears in the Source pane and is selected. Its name is highlighted to indicate that you can edit it, and you see the content you selected in the Content pane, as shown in Figure 8.1.

iTunes attempts to name the playlist by looking for a common denominator in the group of items you selected. For example, if you select songs from the same artist, that artist's name is the playlist's initial name.

FIGURE 8.1   When you create a playlist based on selected content, you see that content as soon as the playlist exists.

Similarly, if you select songs from the same album, the playlist's name is the artist's and album's names. Sometimes iTunes picks an appropriate name, and sometimes it doesn't.

While the playlist name is highlighted, edit the name as needed and then press **Enter** (Windows) or **Return** (Mac). The playlist is ready for you to add more content, organize, and so on.

Adding Content to a Playlist

The whole point of creating a playlist is to add content to it. Whether you create an empty playlist or one that already has some songs in it, the steps to add content to the playlist are the same:

1. Double-click the playlist's icon in the Source pane. It opens in a separate window whose title is the name of the playlist.

2. Position the playlist's window so that you can see it and the iTunes window.

3. In the iTunes window, browse or search for content you want to add to the playlist. You can move content from any source, including other playlists, into a playlist.

4. Select the items you want to add to the playlist and drag them onto the playlist's window (see Figure 8.2). As you drag, the pointer becomes the add (+) icon and shows the number of items you are moving. When you release the mouse button, the content is added to the playlist.

FIGURE 8.2   Here you see me adding the highlighted items from the iTunes window in the foreground to the playlist's window that is open in the background; the number attached to the pointer indicates how many items I'm adding to the playlist.

5. Repeat steps 3 and 4 until you have added all the content you want to include in the playlist. The playlist is ready for you to organize and use.

Click the playlist's window to bring it to the front. You see its contents in a window that offers the same tools as the iTunes window. For example, you can use the Browser in it, play the content with the playback controls, sort the list, change views, and so on. Information about the playlist, such as its playing time, appears in the Source Information area at the bottom of the iTunes window.

> TIP: **Separate Window Optional**
>
> You don't have to perform step 1. Instead, you can drag content from the Content pane onto the playlist's icon in the Source pane. When you move the content over the playlist's icon, the playlist is highlighted and you see the add (+) pointer showing the number of items you are adding. Release the mouse button and the content is added to the playlist. This works great, but having the playlist open in a separate window is often easier.

Removing Songs from a Playlist

If you decide you don't want one or more tracks included in a playlist, select the tracks you want to remove and press the **Delete** key. A warning prompt appears. Click **Yes** and the tracks are deleted from the playlist. (If you don't want to be prompted each time you delete tracks from a playlist, check the **Do not ask me again** check box.)

Because items in a playlist are only pointers to content, when you delete content from a playlist, it isn't deleted from the Library; it is only removed from the playlist.

Setting the Order in Which a Playlist's Content Plays

The order in which a playlist's items play is determined by the order in which they appear in the Content pane. (The first track is the one at the top of the window, the second is the next one down, and so on. The exception to this is when you play a playlist in Shuffle mode, in which case, the playback order is randomized.) When the list is sorted by the Track Number column (which is the unlabeled column that always appears at the left edge of the window), you can drag tracks higher on the list to make them play earlier or down in the list to make them play later. You can move tracks individually, or you can select multiple tracks and move them at the same time.

Just like the Content pane in the iTunes window, you can also change the order in which tracks play by sorting the playlist by its columns.

When you re-sort by the Track Number column, the order returns to the previous order it was in when last sorted by the Track Number column. So, you don't lose any manual ordering you've done because you sort by one of the other columns; you can always return to that order by sorting by Track Number again.

Deleting a Playlist

If you decide you no longer want a playlist, you can delete it by selecting the playlist on the Source list and pressing the Delete key. A prompt appears; click Delete and the playlist is removed from the Source list. (Be sure to check the **Do not ask me again** check box if you don't want to be prompted in the future.) Again, because playlists store only pointers to content, deleting a playlist doesn't impact its content in your Library; it only removes the playlist from the Source pane and deletes the pointers to the content that was included in the playlist.

Creating and Managing Smart Playlists

The basic purpose of a smart playlist is the same as a playlist: to contain a collection of content you can listen to and watch, put on mobile device, and so on. However, the path smart playlists take to this end is completely different from playlists. Instead of choosing specific content as you do for a playlist, you tell iTunes the kind of content you want in your smart playlist, and it chooses the content of the playlist for you.

For example, suppose you want to create a playlist that contains all your classical music. Instead of picking out all the songs in your Library that have the classical genre (as you would do to create a playlist), you can use a smart playlist to tell iTunes to include all music with Classical as the Genre tag. iTunes gathers all the music that has that genre and places it in a smart playlist.

> CAUTION: **Tags and Smart Playlists**
>
> Creating smart playlists depends on your content being properly tagged with information, such as genre, artist, song names, and so on. Sometimes content you add to your Library, such as by MP3 files that are stored on your hard drive, won't have all this information. Before you get going with smart playlists, make sure you have your content properly labeled and categorized using the techniques you learned in Lesson 7, "Tagging iTunes Content."

Creating Smart Playlists

You create a smart playlist by defining a set of rules based on any number of tags. After you have selected the rules for the smart playlist, iTunes chooses content with matching tags and places them in the playlist.

One of the really cool things about smart playlists is that they can be dynamic; iTunes calls this live updating. When a smart playlist is set to be live, iTunes changes its contents over time to match changes to the content in your Library. If you add content with tags specified for the smart playlist or change the tags on existing content so that they match, the content is added to the smart playlist automatically. This makes smart playlists great for grouping content so that it reflects changes to your Library. (If this feature isn't enabled for a smart playlist, that playlist contains only the content that met the rules at the time the playlist was created.)

You can include multiple rules for a playlist, such as artist, genre, and so on. You can also create multiple sets of rules, with each set containing one or more rules.

You link multiple rules by the logical expression All or Any. If you use an All logical expression, all the rules must be true for content to be included in the smart playlist. If you use the Any option, only one of the rules has to be met for content to be included in the smart playlist.

You can create a smart playlist by completing the following steps:

1. Select **File**, **New Smart Playlist** or hold down the Shift (Windows) or Option (Mac) key and click the **Create Playlist** button (which becomes the Create New Smart Playlist button when the Shift or Option key is pressed down).

You see the Smart Playlist dialog box. It contains menus and boxes that you use to choose and define the rules for content to be included and check boxes and menus to set properties for the smart playlist. Initially, there is only one rule, but you can add as many rules as you want.

TIP: **Creating Smart Playlists**

You can also create a new smart playlist by pressing **Ctrl+Alt+N** (Windows) or **Option+Cmd+N** (Mac).

---

2. Select the first tag on which you want the rule to be based in the Tag menu, which is on the far left in the dialog box. For example, you can select Artist, Genre, Rating, or Year, among many others. The Operand menu, which is to the right of the Tag menu, is updated so that it is applicable to the tag you selected. For example, if you select Artist, the Operand menu will include Contains, does not contain, is, is not, starts with, and ends with. You see other menus and boxes relevant to the tag you selected, too. For example, if you choose the Media Kind tag, you see two menus, but no boxes.

3. Select the operand you want to use from the Operand menu. For example, if you want to match data exactly, select **is**. If you want the rule to be looser, select **contains**. The options you have depend on the tag you select.

4. Type or select the rule's condition you want to match in the Rule box or menu. As you type, iTunes tries to match what you are typing based on content in your Library. The more you type, the more specific the rule is. The options you have depend on the specific tag you include in the rule.

As an example, if you select Artist as the tag, select **contains** as the operand, and type **Elvis**, the rule looks for content where the Artist tag contains Elvis and finds all content where the Artist tag is Elvis, Elvis Presley, Elvis Costello, Elvisiocity, and so on. If you type **Elvis Presley** in the Rule box and select the **contains** operand, iTunes includes content whose artist includes Elvis

Presley, such as Elvis Presley, Elvis Presley and His Backup Band, and so on.

The example shown in Figure 8.3 has one rule based on the Artist tag—so far.

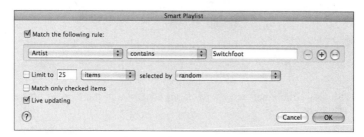

FIGURE 8.3   At this point, this smart playlist will contain any content with Switchfoot as part of the Artist tag.

5. To add another rule to the smart playlist, click the **Add Rule** button (+). A new, empty rule appears under the first rule. At the top of the dialog box, the All or Any menu also appears.

6. Select the tag the new rule uses. For example, if you want to include songs from a specific genre, select **Genre** from the menu.

7. Select the operand you want to use from the Operand menu, such as contains, is, and so on.

8. Type the rule you want to match in the Rule box or select the rule from the Rule menu. As an example, if you select **Genre**, type the genre from which the content in the playlist should come. As you type, iTunes tries to match the genre you type with those in your Library.

9. Repeat steps 5 through 8 to add more rules to the playlist until you have all the rules you want to include.

10. Choose **any** from the Match menu to include content if any of the rules are true; choose **all** if all the rules must be true. The example shown in Figure 8.4 now has multiple rules, with each rule based on the Artist tag. You can mix and match tags among a set of rules, too.

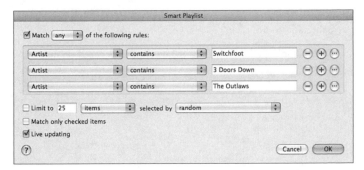

FIGURE 8.4   This smart playlist finds any content with the listed artists as the Artist tag.

11. To add a set of rules, click the **Add Set of Rules** button (**...**). The all/any menu appears along with an indented rule, which is the first rule in the set you are creating.

12. Use the tools in the rule set to define each rule you want to include. These work the same as adding individual rules.

13. Choose **any** for the rule set if content meeting any of the rules should be included; choose **all** if all of the rules in the set must be met.

As you add individual rules and rule sets, predicting the results of a smart playlist gets more complicated. However, if you carefully think about each rule and how the rules are connected, you can get pretty accurate. As an example, try to predict the results of the smart playlist shown in Figure 8.5.

The example playlist finds any content with the following terms included in the Artist tag: Switchfoot, 3 Doors Down, and The Outlaws. These are defined by the top three rules. The rule set finds content only if (because all is selected on the menu at the top of the rule set) that content's Artist tag contains Lynyrd Skynyrd, is rated with 4 or 5 stars, and is from the Rock genre. Because any is selected on the top menu, content that meets any of the three individual rules or the rule set is included.

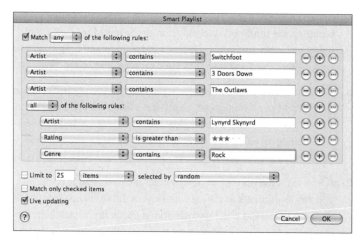

FIGURE 8.5 This smart playlist now has three individual rules and one rule set.

TIP: **Removing Rules**

If you want to remove a rule, click the **Remove** button (-) for the rule you want to remove. To remove a rule set, remove all of its rules.

---

14. If you want to limit the amount of content in the playlist, check the **Limit to** check box; if you don't want to set a limit on the playlist's content, leave the check box unchecked and skip to step 18.

15. Select the attribute by which you want to limit the playlist in the first menu. Your choices include the amount of time the playlist will play (minutes or hours), the size of the files the playlist contains (MB or GB), or the number of items (items).

16. Type the amount appropriate for the limit you select in the Limit To box. For example, if you select GB on the menu, type the maximum size for the playlist in the box. This proves especially useful for creating playlist to move content onto a portable device or disc because you can configure the playlist to use a specific amount of the device's or disc's storage space.

17. Select how you want iTunes to choose the content it includes based on the limit you selected from the Selected by menu. This menu has many options, including randomly, based on rating, when the content was added to your Library, and so on.

18. If you want the playlist to include only songs whose check box in the Content pane is checked, check the **Match only checked items** check box. If you leave this check box unchecked, iTunes will include all items that meet the playlist's rules, even if you have unchecked their check boxes in the Content pane.

19. If you want the playlist to be dynamic, meaning that iTunes updates its contents as the content in your Library changes, check the **Live updating** check box. If you uncheck this check box, the playlist includes only those items that meet the playlist's rules when you create it.

20. Click **OK** to create the playlist. You move to the Source pane, the smart playlist is created and selected, and its name is ready for you to edit. Also, the content in your Library that matches the playlist's rules is added to it, and the current contents of the playlist are shown in the Content pane.

21. Type the playlist's name and press **Enter** (Windows) or **Return** (Mac). The smart playlist is complete.

Building a smart playlist based on just a few rules is simple. Creating sophisticated smart playlists with multiple rules and rule sets takes some practice. To build a complex smart playlist, add rules or rules sets one at a time and check the results each time you add the rule or rule set by clicking **OK** and looking at the contents of the playlist in the Content pane. This tells you whether the most recent rule or rule set has the effect you intend. If not, change the smart playlist, as described in the next section, to correct its rules and rule sets before adding the next rule or rule set.

Over time and with practice, you get the hang of how smart playlist rules and rule sets work and are able to get iTunes to create just about any set of content you want.

Changing Smart Playlists

To change the contents of a smart playlist, you change the smart playlist's rules; iTunes updates the contents of the playlist based on the changes you make to its rules.

Select the smart playlist in the Source pane and choose **File, Edit Smart Playlist**. The Smart Playlist dialog box appears; the title of the dialog box is now the name of the playlist, and the playlist's current rules are shown, as in Figure 8.6.

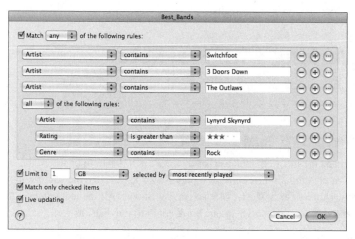

FIGURE 8.6   You can tell I am editing a smart playlist because the playlist's title appears at the top of the dialog box.

Use the techniques in the previous section to change the playlist's rules. You can change existing rules, add new rules or rule sets, remove rules, or change any of the playlist's settings. When you finish making changes, click **OK**. Your changes are saved, and the contents of the playlist are updated to match the current rules.

If live updating is enabled for a playlist, iTunes changes its contents as your Library's content changes. For example, if you download new content that meets the playlist's rules, it is added to the playlist automatically.

You can also change the order in which a smart playlist plays just like a playlist, such as sorting it by clicking a column heading. Over time, the contents of a smart playlist may change if live updating is enabled, which can impact any sorting you apply.

Deleting a Smart Playlist

To delete a smart playlist, select it on the Source list and press **Delete**. Confirm the deletion at the prompt, and the playlist is removed from the Source pane. Of course, this removes only the playlist; it has no effect on the content stored in your Library.

Working with Playlists

After you create playlists, you can work with them in a number of ways, as discussed in the following subsections.

Watching and Listening to Playlists

Perhaps the most obvious use for a playlist is to listen to or watch the content it contains. In this context, a playlist works just like the sources in your Library, such Music, Movies, or TV Shows. All the techniques you learned in lessons earlier in this book apply to playlists, as well.

Select the playlist you want to listen to or watch. Use iTunes browse, search, and other tools to find and organize the content as you want to experience it. Then, play the content using the iTunes playback controls.

Organizing Playlists in Folders

You might end up creating many playlists as time passes. Lots of playlists can clutter up your Source pane, making finding specific content you want more difficult than it should be. Fortunately, you can use folders to keep your playlists organized.

To create folder, choose **File**, **New Playlist Folder**. An empty folder appears in the PLAYLISTS section with its name ready to edit. Type the name for the folder and press **Enter** (Windows) or Return (Mac). The folder is renamed and is moved to its position in the Source pane according to its name. (Folders are listed alphabetically and appear at the top of the PLAYLISTS section of the Source pane.)

You can work with folders in the following ways:

▶ To place a playlist in a folder, drag the playlist onto the folder's icon and release the mouse button. The playlist is stored within the folder. Within folders, playlists are sorted in alphabetic order. All the smart playlists within a folder are grouped at the top of the folder with playlists listed under them.

▶ To expand the contents of a folder, click its right-facing triangle. To collapse the contents again so that you see only the folder icon, click its down-facing triangle. Figure 8.7 shows some collapsed and expanded folders.

FIGURE 8.7 You can expand and collapse folders to see or hide their contents.

▶ You can nest folders to create a hierarchy of folders by dragging one folder onto another one. Or select a folder and choose the **New Playlist Folder** command.

▶ To delete a folder, select it and press **Delete**. If you confirm the action, the folder and all the playlists it contains are deleted. As you expect, none of the content in your Library is impacted.

▶ Double-click a folder to open it in a separate window.

▶ You can see, listen to, or watch a folder's contents as if it is a playlist; the contents of a folder are the contents in each of the playlists it contains. When you select a folder, you see its content in the Content pane, and you can work with folders just like playlists. For example, you can sort their contents, browse and search, and so on.

Using Playlists for Other Purposes

In addition to enjoying the content they contain, you can use playlists for other purposes, such as the following:

▶ Sharing specific content with others on a local network

▶ Burning CDs or other types of discs

▶ Creating collections of content to move onto iPods, iPhones, and iPads

▶ Exporting content outside of iTunes

Using iTunes-Created Playlists

iTunes creates several special playlists for you. These include the Purchased playlists, Genius playlists, and the iTunes DJ.

NOTE: **Default Smart Playlists**

iTunes automatically creates several smart playlists for you; these appear in the PLAYLISTS section, just like playlists you create. You can use them in the same ways, too.

Using the Purchased Playlists

Whenever you download content from the iTunes Store, it (more accurately, pointers to it) is added to the various purchased playlists in the STORE section of the Source pane.

The Purchased playlist contains items you've downloaded from the Store onto your computer. You also see playlists for content that you download from the Store using other devices, such as the iTunes app on an iPhone. Each device has its own playlist, and the playlists are named with the name of the device, such as Purchased on Brad Miser's iPad.

You can use these playlists to quickly access content you've downloaded. And, you can use these playlists just like playlists you create (for instance, to listen to songs you download).

> NOTE: **Device Playlists**
> The purchased playlist for a device appears the first time you sync the device after downloading content to that device.

Working with Genius Playlists

The Genius feature finds music and builds a playlist based on songs that "go with" a specific song. How the Genius selects songs that "sound good" with other songs is a bit of a secret, but it works amazingly well. You can have the Genius build a playlist for you in a couple of ways and then listen to or update it.

Creating and Using Genius Playlists

To create a genius playlist based on the current song, do the following:

1. Find and play a song.

2. Click the **Genius** button in the Information area at the top of the iTunes window or in the lower-right corner of the iTunes window. While the music plays, the Genius playlist is created, and you move to the new playlist where you see the songs that the Genius selected; the song that is currently playing is at the top of the list and is marked with the Speaker icon. At the top of the list

of songs, you see the song on which the playlist is based along with tools you can use to work with the playlist, as shown in Figure 8.8.

FIGURE 8.8   This genius playlist is based on "Dare You to Move."

While you are the playlist's screen, you can do the following:

- ▶ Choose the number of songs you want to include in the playlist from the Limit To menu at the top of the Content pane. You can choose 25, 50, 75, or 100 songs.

- ▶ Refresh the playlist by clicking the **Refresh** button. This causes the Genius to select a new set of songs based on the song on which the playlist is based. How different the refreshed playlist is depends on how many songs "go with" the playlist's song in your Library and how many songs you have included in the playlist.

- ▶ Save the playlist by clicking **Save Playlist**. The playlist is saved with the name of the song on which it is based as the playlist's title.

Your Genius playlists are stored in the GENIUS section of the Source pane. When you select a Genius playlist you've saved, you can work with it just like other playlists you've created. However, you can also change the numbers of songs to which the playlist is limited using its Limit to menu or refresh it by clicking the **Refresh** button.

NOTE: **The Genius Playlist**

The Genius playlist, which is the first entry in the GENIUS section, always contains the most recent Genius playlist you created. Each time you create a new Genius playlist, the contents of the Genius playlist are replaced. You can use the Genius playlist just like the other playlists in the GENIUS section.

You can also delete a Genius playlist just like other playlists—select the playlist you want to delete and press the **Delete** key.

Using Genius Mixes

When you select the Genius Mixes playlist, you see content iTunes has organized for you based on various characteristics of your music, such as genre or vocals, as shown in Figure 8.9. When you hover over a mix, you see the artists contained in the mix and the Play button at the center of the mix's thumbnail. Click the **Play** button to play the music in the mix. While a mix is playing, playback controls appear as you move over its thumbnail.

Using the iTunes DJ

The iTunes DJ is a special playlist that selects songs for you. You choose the source of the music and configure other aspects of the playlist. The DJ then selects and plays songs from this source, mostly randomly. One of the fun things about the DJ is that you can allow other people to request songs remotely using the Remote app on an iPod, iPhone, or iPad.

To use the iTunes DJ, select it in the Source pane. (If you've never used it before, some basic information about it appears; click **Continue** to move into the DJ.)

FIGURE 8.9   Genius mixes contain selections of your music based on different attributes, such as whether the music has vocals.

Configure the DJ by clicking the **Settings** button at the bottom of the iTunes window. The iTunes DJ Settings dialog box appears, as shown in Figure 8.10. On the dialog box, you can configure the following settings:

▶ **Number of songs displayed.** Use the **recently played songs** and **upcoming songs** settings to determine the number of songs shown "before" the current one (meaning they have played) and "after" the current song in the Content pane.

▶ **Play higher rated songs more often.** Check this check box to cause the DJ to choose songs you've rated with more stars "more often" than those you haven't rated or have rated with a lower number of stars.

▶ **Allow remote requests.** Check the **Allow guests to request songs with Remote for iPhone or iPod touch** check box to allow people to request songs using a mobile device. You can also provide a message that people see when they access your DJ.

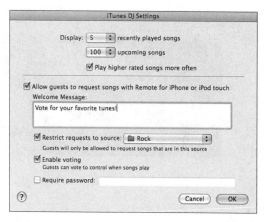

FIGURE 8.10   Use this dialog to configure certain aspects of how the iTunes DJ works.

▶ **Restricts requests to source.** Check this check box and choose a source from the menu to limit the source of music guests can view and request.

▶ **Enable voting.** If you check this check box, guests can vote on the order in which upcoming songs should play.

▶ **Require password.** To require people to enter a password before they can access your DJ, check the **Require password** check box and enter the password in the box.

After you've configured the DJ, select the source of music you want to shuffle on the Source pop-up menu located at the bottom of the iTunes window. You can choose the Music source or any playlist or folder. The Content pane shows the songs the DJ selects. Use the playback controls to start the music playing. The current song is marked with the Speaker icon. Songs that have previously played are shown above the current song, and are grayed out. Upcoming songs appear below the current song, as shown in Figure 8.11.

FIGURE 8.11 The iTunes DJ playlist selects and plays music from the Source you see on the Source menu.

The iTunes DJ playlist plays forever. After it plays a song, it moves one of the recently played songs off that list, moves the song it just played into the recently played section, highlights and plays the next song, and adds another one to the upcoming songs section. This process continues until you stop the music.

You can manually add songs to the iTunes DJ. View a source to find the song you want to add, and then right-click that song. A menu of several options displays, as shown in Figure 8.12. Choose **Play Next in iTunes DJ** to have the song play next, or select **Add to iTunes DJ** to add the song to the beginning of upcoming songs list. The difference between this is that when you choose Play Next in iTunes DJ, the song is the next one played. When you choose Add to iTunes DJ, the song is added to the upcoming list after any other songs that have already been added.

You can have the iTunes DJ refresh the list of upcoming songs by clicking the **Refresh** button. It replaces the current list of upcoming songs with a new one, except for those that have been added manually, which remain on the list.

FIGURE 8.12 The iTunes DJ playlist selects and plays music from the Source you see on the Source menu.

NOTE: **Make a Party**

The iTunes DJ can be a lot of fun when you have a group of people together. People with Apple mobile devices can add songs to the playlist from their devices, making the process much more interactive than just listening to whatever comes next. You learn about using the iTunes DJ for this in Lesson 11, "Streaming Music with Airplay."

Summary

In this lesson, you learned how to create, manage, and use playlists. You also learned about the playlists that iTunes creates for you. In the next lesson, you learn how to move your iTunes content onto other devices.

LESSON 9

Subscribing to and Enjoying Podcasts

In this lesson, you learn how to find, subscribe to, and enjoy audio and video podcasts. You also learn how to configure how podcasts are managed in iTunes.

Understanding Podcasts

Podcasts are radio-like audio or TV-like video you can add to your iTunes Library and listen to or watch them. Podcasts exist for just about any topic you can think of and are created by individuals or organizations. Some podcasts are informative in nature, such as news podcasts, whereas others are for entertainment only.

You add podcasts to your iTunes Library by subscribing to them from the iTunes Store. You can also find thousands more podcasts on a variety of websites; for example, many radio shows also provide their content in podcasts that you can download from the show's website.

Like radio and TV shows, most podcasts are provided in episodes. When you want to be able to listen to or view a podcast, you subscribe to it; subscribing to a podcast causes it to be downloaded to your computer and added to your iTunes Library. You can also choose to download previous episodes if you want to. (You can't subscribe to all podcasts; some are provided as individual files that you download to your computer and then add to your iTunes Library.)

After you have downloaded podcasts, you can listen to or watch them on your computer, move them to an iPod, and so on.

Subscribing to Podcasts in the iTunes Store

You can access and subscribe to thousands of podcasts in the iTunes Store. Most of these podcasts are free. You can preview podcasts before you subscribe to them. Once you subscribe to a podcast, future episodes download to your computer automatically according to your preferences.

Like other content, you can browse or search for podcasts in the iTunes Store. The following steps show you how to find podcasts by browsing:

1. Move into the iTunes Store and click the **Podcasts** tab. You move to the Podcasts home page. You can browse the page to find podcasts or continue with these steps to browse by category.

2. Open the **Podcasts** menu by clicking the downward-facing arrow just to the right of the word "Podcasts," and choose the category you want to browse, such as Business, as shown in Figure 9.1.

FIGURE 9.1   Use the Podcasts menu to browse podcasts by category.

3. Browse the resulting screen to find a podcast of interest to you. Podcasts are grouped into various categories, top lists, types, and so on.

4. To get information about a podcast, click its thumbnail or title. You move to the information screen for that podcast, as shown in Figure 9.2. You see a description of the podcast along with customer reviews and other podcasts that listeners to the one you are viewing have subscribed to.

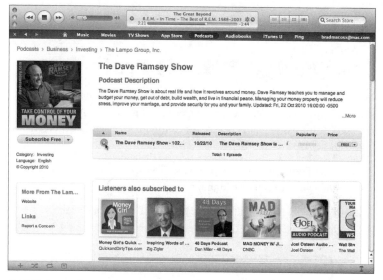

FIGURE 9.2   Use a podcast's information screen to preview or subscribe to it.

5. To preview an episode, hover over the episode number and click the **Play** button. If it is a free podcast, and most are, you can listen to or watch the entire episode. If it has a fee, you hear or see a segment of the episode.

6. To subscribe to the podcast, click the **Subscribe** button, which also indicates how much the subscription costs (free in most cases).

7. In the resulting prompt, click **Subscribe**. You are subscribed to the podcast. The current episodes are downloaded to your Library; future episodes download as they become available (according to preferences you set, as you learn in the next section).

TIP: **Searching for Podcasts**

You can also find podcasts using a power search. Just choose **Podcasts** from the menu, and then configure the rest of the fields and menus to perform the search. This is often the fastest way to find a specific podcast and requires just a little bit of information, such as a partial title for the podcast or its author.

Configuring Podcast Preferences

You can set podcast preferences to determine how iTunes manages your podcasts. You can set default preferences for all podcasts, and you can set preferences for individual podcasts. To configure your podcast preferences, follow these steps:

1. Select **Podcasts** in the Source pane. You see the podcasts to which you are subscribed in the Content pane.

2. Click the **Settings** button at the bottom of the iTunes window. The Podcast Settings dialog appears, as shown in Figure 9.3.

FIGURE 9.3 Configure your preferences to determine how iTunes manages your podcast subscriptions.

3. If **Podcast Defaults** isn't selected on the Settings for menu, choose it. This sets the preferences for all your podcasts unless you override them for a specific podcast.

4. Use the **Check for new episodes** drop-down list to choose how often you want iTunes to check for new episodes. The options are Every Hour, Every Day, Every Week, and Manually. iTunes checks for new episodes according to the timeframe you select— unless you choose **Manually**, in which case you must check for new episodes manually. Just under the Check for new episodes drop-down list, you see when the next check for new episodes will be performed.

5. Use the **When new episodes are available** drop-down list to determine what iTunes does when it finds new episodes of the podcasts to which you are subscribed. Choose **Download the most recent one** if you want only the newest episode to be downloaded. Choose **Download all** if you want all available episodes downloaded. Choose **Do nothing** if you don't any episodes to be downloaded.

6. Use the **Keep** drop-down list to determine whether and when iTunes deletes podcast episodes. Choose **All episodes** if you don't want iTunes to automatically remove any episodes. Select **All unplayed episodes** if you want iTunes to remove episodes you've watched or listened to, or select **Most recent episode** if you want iTunes to keep only the most recent episode even if you haven't listened to or watched all of them. Select **Last x episodes**, where x is 2, 3, 4, 5, or 10, to have iTunes keep only the selected number of episodes.

7. To override the preference settings for an individual podcast, select it from the Settings for drop-down list.

8. Uncheck the **Use Default Settings** check box.

9. Use steps 5 and 6 to configure the podcast's settings.

10. Repeat steps 7 through 9 until you've configure settings for all the podcasts for which you want to override the default settings.

11. Click **OK**. The dialog box closes and your podcast preferences are set.

> TIP: **Finding Podcasts in Other Places**
>
> The iTunes Store is the easiest source of podcasts to use, but it is certainly not the only one. Many websites, particularly those for radio shows, offer podcasts. These usually require a fee to subscribe to them. After you subscribe via the podcast's website, you usually see a link to click to add the podcast to iTunes. From that point forward, these podcasts work just like those that you subscribe to in the iTunes Store. You can sometimes download podcasts directly from a website without going through a subscription process. You can manually add the podcast's files to your iTunes Library using the Add to Library commands on the File menu.

Listening to, Watching, and Managing Podcasts

After you have subscribed to podcasts, you can listen to or watch them in iTunes, and you can move them onto a mobile device, such as an iPod. You can also manage the podcasts to which you have subscribed.

To work with your podcasts, click **Podcasts** on the Source list. You see the podcasts to which you have subscribed in the Content pane, as shown in Figure 9.4.

The following list describes how you can work with podcasts:

▶ To see all the episodes available for a podcast, click its right-facing triangle. All the available episodes are shown. The episodes that have been downloaded to your computer but that you haven't listened to or watched yet have a blue dot next to them. Those that you have started listening to or watching have a partially filled blue dot; the dot disappears when you've listened to or watched the entire episode. Those that haven't been downloaded yet are grayed out, and the Get button is shown.

▶ To collapse a podcast so that you see only its title, click its downward-facing triangle.

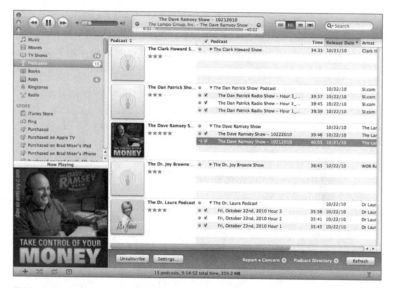

FIGURE 9.4 Use the Podcasts source to work with the podcasts to which you're subscribed.

> NOTE: **No Sorting Podcast Episodes**
>
> You can't choose the column by which the Podcast source is sorted; podcasts are listed in alphabetic order. Episodes of a podcast are always sorted by release date. You can change the sort order, however, so that episodes of podcasts are listed from oldest to newest or vice versa.

▶ To download an episode, click its **Get** button. To download all the episodes for a podcast, click its **Get All** button. The episodes are downloaded to your computer. When that process is complete, the new episodes are marked with a blue dot, and you can listen to or watch them.

▶ To play an episode of a podcast, select it and click the **Play** button. The iTunes playback controls work similarly to how they do for other types of content.

▶ Click the **Podcast Directory** link at the bottom of the Content pane to move to the Podcast home page in the iTunes Store.

▶ Set the Keep preference so that iTunes automatically keeps or deletes the episodes for each podcast. For example, choose the **All Unplayed Episodes** option if you want iTunes to automatically delete episodes after you listen to or watch them.

▶ To delete an episode from your Library (whether it's been downloaded), select it and press the Delete key. If the file has been downloaded to your Library, click the **Move to Recycle Bin** (Windows) or **Move to Trash** (Mac) button to delete the podcasts files from your computer and from the Library or the **Keep Files** button to remove the podcast from your Library but leave its files on your computer.

▶ If it's been awhile since you listened to or watched episodes of a subscribed-to podcast, iTunes stops downloading episodes of that podcast and marks it with an exclamation point icon. When you click that icon, you see a message telling you this has happened. You can click the icon again to have episodes of the podcast downloaded to your computer again.

▶ To unsubscribe from a podcast, select the podcast (not an individual episode) and click the **Unsubscribe** button. Episodes of the podcast will no longer be downloaded to your computer, although episodes that you have downloaded remain in your Library and you can listen to or watch them or delete them. You can subscribe again by clicking the **Subscribe** button that appears next to a podcast to which you used to be subscribed. If you don't regularly listen to a podcast, you should unsubscribe from it so that you aren't wasting disk space.

▶ To delete a podcast from your Library, select it and press the Delete key. Click the **Move to Recycle Bin** (Windows) or **Move to Trash** (Mac) button to delete the podcasts files from your computer and from the Library or the **Keep Files** button to remove the podcast from your Library but leave its files on your computer.

► Click the **Refresh** button to refresh the list of episodes available for each podcast to which you are subscribed. The podcasts' episodes are downloaded to your computer according to your podcast preferences. And episodes are removed based on your Keep preference. (For example, if you've elected to keep only unplayed episodes, all the episodes you've listened to or watched will be deleted.)

► If a podcast has an Exclamation Point icon next to it, that podcast has a problem, such as no content being available. If you want to report the problem, select the podcast and click the **Report a Concern** link. This is available only for podcasts that are available in the iTunes Store. If the Exclamation Point icon appears next to an episode, but the Get button is enabled, there was a problem downloading that episode. Click the **Get** button to try to download it again.

Summary

In this lesson, you learned how to take advantage of the thousands of audio and video podcasts available to you. In the next lesson, you learn how to add your iTunes content to other devices.

LESSON 10

Moving iTunes Content onto iPods, iPhones, and iPads

In this lesson, you learn how to move content from your iTunes Library onto iPhones, iPods, and iPads. You also learn how to use iTunes to manage the software that runs these devices.

Understanding Syncing

Apple "i" devices are great ways to enjoy your iTunes content away from your computer. To move iTunes content onto one of these devices, you sync the device with your computer. During the sync process, iTunes copies the content you select onto the device; you configure the content that is moved onto the device through tabs, with a tab for each type of content the device you are syncing supports. You can choose to sync all the various types of content onto a device or you can choose a subset of your content to move onto a device. On devices that support apps, email, and so on, you can also copy the related content and information onto the device.

One of the great things about iTunes is that it manages all the complexity of syncing for you. All you do is make selections to indicate the content and other information you want to move onto a device; iTunes then copies that information onto the device each time you connect it to your computer.

Syncing Content on iPods, iPhones, and iPads

When you connect an iPod, iPhone, or iPad to your computer, iTunes recognizes the device and shows it in the DEVICES section of the Source pane. When you select the device, you see buttons at the top of the Content pane. Each button enables you to configure a specific type of content or information to copy onto the device.

NOTE: **Storage Space**

In many cases, you have more content in your iTunes Library than fits on a device. Because of this, you need to choose subsets of your content to include in the sync process. Playlists are ideal ways to define collections of content that you want to have available to you on your iPod, iPhone, or iPad. You can create playlists of specific sizes to ensure the content you want fits into the device's available storage space. You learned all about playlists in Lesson 8.

Each device (and each generation of device) may support different kinds of content. Fortunately, you don't have to worry about the details of this because iTunes determines the types of content compatible with the connected device and configures itself accordingly. For example, compare the options available for an iPod nano shown in Figure 10.1 to those available for an iPad shown in Figure 10.2.

Regardless of the type of device you have, the process of syncing is similar. Following are the general steps you use to configure a sync:

1. Connect the device to your computer and select the device in the Source pane.

2. Click the second button at the top of the Content pane; what this is depends on the device. For example, for an iPad, click **Info**, but for an iPod nano, it is **Music**.

3. Use the **Sync** check boxes to include or exclude content when you sync the device. For example, on the Music screen, you see the Sync Music check box. When you check this check box, the other controls that you use to select the specific music you want to move onto the device become active.

4. Use the selection tools to include specific content in the sync process. The tools available depend on the type of content you are configuring. Using Music as an example, you can click the **Entire music library** radio button to try to sync all your music or the **Selected playlists**, artists, albums, and genres button to select a subset of your music.

FIGURE 10.1 Here you see the sync options for an iPod nano.

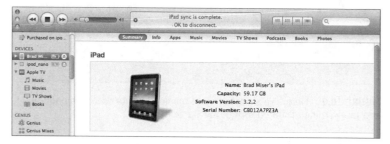

FIGURE 10.2 Because this iPad supports more types of content, it has more sync options.

5. When you choose a subset of the content to sync (if you select the Entire option, you don't perform this step), use the other tools to choose the portion of your Library you want to move onto the device. Continuing with the Music example, you can choose music by selecting playlists, artists, genres, or albums to include by checking each item's check box.

6. Select the next button at the top of the screen to move into the next content type, such as Movies.

7. Repeat steps 3 through 5 to configure the content of that type you want to include.

8. Repeat steps 6 and 7 until you configure all the areas the device supports. As you add content, monitor the device's available memory using the gauge at the bottom of the screen, as shown in Figure 10.3. When you include more content in the sync than fits onto the device, you see the Warning icon and the amount of content selected that is beyond the capacity of the device. You should remove content until it fits onto the device. However, you can proceed with the sync, and iTunes fits as much of the selected content onto the device as it can. The problem with doing so is that you aren't sure which content gets moved, and so you won't be sure what content is available on the device.

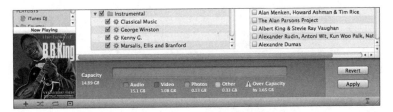

FIGURE 10.3 Here, I've selected more music than fits onto this nano and see the warning at the bottom of the Capacity gauge.

9. When you're ready to copy the content, click **Apply**. The sync configuration is saved for the device so that the next time you connect it iTunes syncs it with the same settings automatically. The sync process starts, and you can monitor it in the Information area at the top of the iTunes window.

10. When the process completes, you can eject and disconnect the device. The content you synced is ready for you to work with on the device. Each time you connect the device, it is automatically synced using the same settings (until you change them).

NOTE: **Sync Versus Apply**

Whenever you make changes to the sync settings for a device, the Apply button appears indicating you can apply your changes and resync the device with the new settings. Then next time you connect the device, you see the Sync button instead. When you click this, the sync occurs using the last sync settings. As soon as you change at least one setting, the Sync button becomes Apply again.

Managing Software on iPods, iPhones, and iPads

iPods, iPhones, and iPads are complex devices and operate through the iOS operating system software. Each type and generation of device supports its particular functionality through a specific version of the iOS. iTunes manages this complexity for you. For example, it enables you to ensure you have the most current version of the iOS, update your software to the current version of the iOS, and restore the software in the event the device experiences problems.

To work with the operating system software on one of the devices, you use the Summary screen. On the Summary screen, you can perform the following actions, as shown in Figure 10.4:

- ▶ **Check for Update.** Click this button to see whether a newer version of the operating system is available. If the device is using the current version, you see a message telling you so. If a newer version is available, you're prompted to download and install it.

- ▶ **Update.** When iTunes has determined a newer version of the operating system is available, click this button to download (if required) and install it. Follow the onscreen prompts to complete the process.

FIGURE 10.4   Use the Summary screen to update or restore a device's operating system software.

▶ **Restore.** If a device is not working properly, use this button to download and install the current version of the operating system. This overwrites the current operating system software, which corrects many problems. You can also choose to restore it as a new device or using the backups from a previous sync.

NOTE: **Content Versus Software**

Even when you restore a device, your iTunes content is safe because it is stored in the iTunes Library. When the restore process completes, the devices syncs according to the settings you last used for it (assuming you choose the Restore from backup option) and your content is also restored in the device. The net effect is that the device's operating system is restored to the current version, but your content is as it was before the restore.

Summary

In this lesson, you learned how to move content in your iTunes Library onto Apple's mobile devices and to work with the operating system on your devices. In the next lesson, you learn how to use an AirPlay network.

LESSON 11

Streaming Music with AirPlay

In this lesson, you learn how to use AirPlay to broadcast your iTunes music so that you can enjoy it in multiple locations. You also learn how you can use iPods, iPhones, and iPads as remote controls for music playback.

Understanding AirPlay

AirPlay enables you to stream your iTunes music over a wireless network to AirPort Express Base Stations with speakers connected to them. This enables you to listen to your iTunes music wherever you have a base station/speaker combination installed. You can control music playback using iTunes, including which speakers are active, but it's even better when you use an iPhone, iPod, or iPad as a remote control.

Creating an AirPlay Network

To use AirPlay to stream music, you need a wireless network with one or more AirPort Express Base Stations connected to speakers or to other devices, such as a receiver, that can play music. You can use multiple base station/speaker pairs in different rooms or other locations. As long as a base station is connected to your wireless network, iTunes can stream music to it.

There are multiple configurations for an AirPlay network, and the details of setting up and managing a wireless network are beyond the scope of this book. However, the general steps to create an AirPlay network follow:

▶ **Install and configure a wireless hub/router to provide a wireless network.** You can use an Apple Time Capsule, AirPort

Extreme Base Station, Apple AirPort Express Base Station, or other brand of wireless router. Configure the router to provide the wireless network, which typically includes a connection to the Internet.

▶ **Install and configure AirPort Express Base Stations.** Configure your AirPort Base Stations to connect to your wireless network. You can connect them as clients, or you can use them to extend the range of your network. You use the AirPort Utility software to configure the base stations on your network.

NOTE: **Need Help with AirPort?**

For more information on Apple AirPort, see www.apple.com/wifi/.

▶ **Connect speakers to the AirPort Express Base Stations.** You can directly connect powered speakers to the base station speaker ports, or you can connect the speaker port of the base station to the input of another system, such as a receiver. You can use analog or digital connections to a speaker system. (To connect digitally, you need to use a cable with a Toslink adapter to connect to the base station's speaker port.) You can mix and match types, too, so you might have some base stations directly connected to speakers and others that feed into another playback device.

▶ **Configure iTunes to use the AirPlay network.** Open the iTunes Preferences dialog and click the **Devices** tab, as shown in Figure 11.1. Check the **Look for remote speakers connected with AirPlay** check box to activate AirPlay. If you want devices connected to the base stations to be able to control iTunes, check the **Allow iTunes control from remote speakers** check box; some devices that you can use are designed to work with iTunes, and this setting enables them to control iTunes. To be able to control iTunes with devices running the Remote app, check the **Look for iPod touch, iPhone and iPad Remotes** check box. Click **OK** to save your settings.

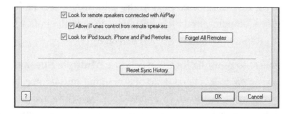

FIGURE 11.1   Configure iTunes to use AirPlay on the Devices tab of the iTunes Preferences dialog box.

Controlling an AirPlay Network with iTunes

Streaming music with iTunes is simple. Select and play the music you want to stream. You do this just as when you are listening to music on your computer.

Then, configure the speakers/locations to which you want to stream music. When you enable AirPlay, you see the Choose Speakers button in the lower-right corner of the iTunes window, as shown in Figure 11.2. When you click this, a menu showing each device capable of streaming music appears. These can be base stations with speakers, Apple TVs, and so on—you also see My Computer, which is the computer iTunes is running on.

Choose Speaker button

FIGURE 11.2   When you enable AirPlay, the Choose Speaker button appears; click it to select speakers to stream music to.

To stream music to a single location, choose it on the menu; it's marked with the check mark to show you it is the current device. The menu closes, and you see the device selected next to the Choose Speaker button (unless you select My Computer, in which case you see only the button). The music begins to play on the device you selected.

To stream music to multiple locations, choose **Multiple Speakers**. A dialog box showing each device capable of streaming music appears along with various controls, as shown in Figure 11.3. To send music to a device, check the device's check box; to stop music streaming to a device, uncheck its check box. To set the main volume level, meaning the level set in iTunes, use the **Master Volume** slider at the top of the dialog box. Then, set the relative volume for each device using its **Volume** slider. For example, you might have some devices that play louder than your computer's audio setup does and want a lower volume, or one device might be located in a louder location and so needs a higher volume.

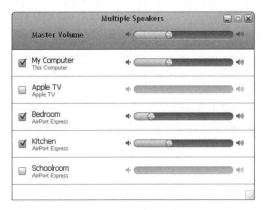

FIGURE 11.3   You can control which devices music streams to and the relative volume level of each.

Using an iPod, iPhone, or iPad as a Remote Control

Controlling streamed music with iTunes on a computer is okay, but it can be inconvenient to go back to your computer to make changes to the music. If you have an iPod touch, iPhone, or iPad, you can use the Remote app to control streaming music from your device.

Connecting Devices to Your iTunes Library

To get started, download and install Apple's Remote app on your device. You can do this by accessing the App Store via iTunes, downloading the Remote app, and then syncing the app onto your device. Or you can use the App Store app to download and install the Remote app.

To enable the device to control your music, you need to connect the device to your iTunes Library. Launch the Remote app on your device and tap the **Choose a Library** button. Tap **Add an iTunes Library**. You see the Add Library screen that presents a four-digit passcode that you enter in iTunes.

Go back into iTunes and select the device you are setting up in the Source pane. Enter the four-digit passcode from the Remote app. If you entered the correct passcode, iTunes connects to the device; click **OK**. (If you see an error message, re-enter the passcode.) Once the passcode is accepted, the device connects to your Library and can control iTunes.

Using the Remote App to Control iTunes

When you launch the Remote app, it connects to your iTunes Library and you can control iTunes using the app's controls, just as if you were sitting at your computer. The Remote app provides lots of options, although it looks different on iPods/iPhones than on an iPad, as you see if you compare Figures 11.4 and 11.5. Functions you can control include the following:

- ▶ **Browse for, search for, and select content to play.** In the iPad version, you see a Source pane that works just like the one in iTunes does. In the iPod/iPhone version, you use the buttons at the bottom of the screen to choose and browse sources. Both versions enable you to search for content. Tap the content to play it.

- ▶ **Playback controls.** Use the familiar buttons to control playback.

- ▶ **Configure speakers.** You can choose which locations music streams to by tapping the Speaker icon. The resulting menu on an iPad or screen on an iPod or iPhone presents the locations available, and you can configure them just as you can when you use iTunes. Tap **Single** to configure locations using the same settings or **Multiple** to apply different volume levels to each.

FIGURE 11.4   Here is the Remote app on an iPad.

FIGURE 11.5   Here are two screens in the Remote app on an iPhone.

▶ **Use the Genius.** Tap the **Genius** button to generate and to create and listen to Genius playlists.

▶ **Create playlists.** Tap the **Create Playlist** button (+) in the iPad version or the **New** button on the Playlists screen of the iPod/iPhone version to create playlists in your iTunes Library.

Using the iTunes DJ Remotely

In Lesson 8, "Creating and Using Playlists," you learned about the iTunes DJ playlist. People with iPods, iPhones, or iPads within range of your network can request music in the iTunes DJ. (If the device is connected to your iTunes Library as in the previous section, it can control the iTunes DJ directly. This section is for guest access.) Select, configure, and play the iTunes DJ on your computer.

To gain access to your iTunes DJ, a guest launches the Remote app and taps the name of your Library in the iTunes DJ section. If required, the guest enters the password. Once the DJ is accessed, the app displays the current and upcoming songs, as shown on the left in Figure 11.6.

To vote for a song, the guest taps the song so that its Heart icon becomes red. iTunes registers the vote for the song and moves it up the playlist. Each vote a song gets moves it higher on the list, and the next song that plays is the one with the most votes.

Guests can also request specific songs by tapping the **Request a Song** button. They see the Request a Song screen, as shown on the right in Figure 11.6. They can browse or search for the song they want to request. When they tap a song, it receives a vote and moves onto or up the playlist according to the number of votes that song has received.

FIGURE 11.6   Guests can vote for songs as on the left or request specific songs as on the right.

NOTE: **Controlling iTunes with Other Devices**

Some devices you can use to stream content from your Library can also control iTunes, assuming you enable the preference to allow this. These devices present various kinds and amounts of control, from the most basic being simple playback controls to those providing full control, such as selecting the content to play (as you can with the Remote app).

Summary

In this lesson, you learned how to use AirPlay to broadcast your iTunes music to multiple locations. In the next lesson, you learn how to share your iTunes content on a local network.

Sharing iTunes Content on a Local Network

In this lesson, you learn how to share iTunes content on a local network. Sharing includes accessing content in a different Library or importing it from one Library to another one to add the content there.

Understanding Sharing

If two or more computers are connected via a local network—and such networks are common these days—you can share the content in your iTunes Library with other iTunes users on your network. They can listen to or watch your content as if it were stored in their own libraries. Of course, assuming other folks on your network are also generous, you can enjoy content they share with you, as well.

There are two ways to share: You can allow other iTunes users to only listen to or watch your content, or you can allow people to import your content into their libraries. Once imported, they can use that content just like other content stored there. Of course, you can do the same with content shared with you.

Windows and Macintosh users can share content with each other on networks that include both kinds of computers.

Sharing Your Content

When you share content, you have two options. You can share your entire Library, or you can share only selected playlists when you want to allow people to access some (but not all) of your content. To configure iTunes to share, complete the following steps:

1. Open the iTunes Preferences dialog box and click the **Sharing** pane, as shown in Figure 12.1.

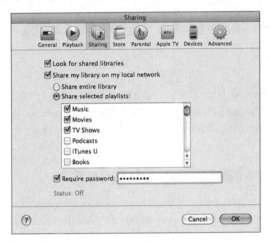

FIGURE 12.1   Use the Sharing pane to allow other people on your network to enjoy your iTunes content on their computers.

2. To enable sharing on your computer, check the **Share my library on my local network** check box.

3. To share your entire Library, click the **Share entire library** radio button and skip to step 5; to share only specific playlists, click the **Share selected playlists** radio button and move to the next step.

4. Check the check box next to each playlist you want to share. You can scroll through the list of available playlists using the scrollbar located on the right side of the list of available playlists.

NOTE: **Playlists?**

In the context of sharing, everything in your Source pane is considered a playlist, including the Music, Movies, TV Shows, and other categories of your Library.

---

5. If you want to require that people enter a password before they can access content you share, check the **Require password**

check box and enter the password they will have to use in the box. This is especially useful when you are on a large network and don't want everyone to be able to access your content.

6. Click **OK**. A prompt reminds you that sharing is for personal use only. (Personal use is just what it sounds like; for you to enjoy for yourself and not for business or other purposes.)

7. Click **OK** to clear the prompt. The content you selected to share becomes available to other iTunes users on your network.

8. If you require a password to let others access your content, provide them with the password you created.

NOTE: **Changes**

If you make changes to the sharing configuration in iTunes while other people are accessing your Library, such as requiring a password, those users might have to restart their iTunes to be able to access your content again.

You can monitor how many people are using the content you are sharing by opening the Sharing pane of the iTunes Preferences dialog box. At the bottom of the pane, you see the current status of sharing (On or Off) and how many users are currently connected to your Library.

NOTE: **iTunes Must Be Running to Share**

It probably goes without saying, but I'll say it anyway: If the computer sharing content stops running or if iTunes on that computer is closed (such as when the user logs out), the shared content source disappears and is no longer accessible. If you share content with others, keep iTunes running as much as you can.

Accessing Shared Content

Two steps are required to access content being shared with you. The first one, which must be done only once, is to tell iTunes to look for any content being shared. The second one is to access the shared content.

NOTE: **No Folders?**

In the context of sharing, iTunes ignores folders. So, you see all playlists on the same list regardless of whether they are stored in folders in the shared source. Also, you can't see album artwork for shared content.

Configuring iTunes to Look for Shared Content

To have iTunes look across the network and identify content that is available to you, open the Sharing pane of the iTunes Preferences dialog box. Check the **Look for shared libraries** check box and click **OK**, as shown in Figure 12.1.

When you return to the iTunes window, you see content that is being shared with you in the Shared section in your Source pane.

Listening to or Watching Shared Content

Is the Shared section, you see each shared Library that you can access. Libraries protected with a password have the lock icon; you need to know the password to be able to work with these shared sources. Libraries that don't require a password have an icon with a musical note inside it.

To access a shared source, select it in the Source pane. If it is password protected, enter its password at the prompt, check the **Remember password** check box (so that you don't have to enter the password again), and click **OK**. The Library you selected is loaded into iTunes; you see its content in the Content pane, and in the Source pane you see a triangle next to the shared Library along with the Eject button, as shown in Figure 12.2.

You can work with shared items in the following ways:

▶ To see all the sources being shared under a source, click its triangle. The source expands, and you see its shared Library sources, such as Music, Movies, and so on, just under the source's name. Underneath these, you see the Playlists folder that contains the individual playlists being shared; click the Playlists folder's triangle to expand its contents. You see each of the shared playlists.

▶ To browse the content in a shared item, select it. The Content
pane presents the contents in the List view. (You can't use any of
the other views when you are working with shared content.)

▶ Except for not being able to change views, you can browse and
organize the lists of shared content, just as you can content in
your Library. For example, you can reorganize columns, use the
view options to add columns, and so on. iTunes remembers view
settings for each shared source, so your configuration is saved
and used the next time you work with the same source.

▶ You can select and play shared content just like content in your
own Library.

▶ When you no longer want to use a shared source, click its **Eject**
button. The source remains in the Source pane as long as it continues to be shared, but the triangle next to it disappears, as does
the Eject button, indicating the source has to be loaded again
when you want to work with it.

FIGURE 12.2   The Shared section of the Source pane shows all libraries
being shared on your network.

CAUTION: **Authorization Required**

If shared content is protected with digital rights management (DRM), you're prompted to enter the account information associated with the iTunes Store account that was used to purchase that content. You must be able to enter the account name and password when prompted to be able to listen to or watch this content.

Using Home Sharing to Import Content Between Libraries

When you share content on a network, others can only listen to or watch that content when your computer is running and iTunes is open. And, the use of shared content is limited in other ways, such as being able to choose different views and so on. In addition to sharing content, you can also allow others to import content from your Library, at which point it becomes part of the other person's Library, as if they were downloading it from the iTunes Store or importing it from a CD. This functionality is called Home Sharing.

You can use Home Sharing to import items from up to five other iTunes Libraries. To use Home Sharing, you must have an iTunes Store account (Apple ID).

To enable Home Sharing, go to the computer on which you want to enable content to be imported or provide your Apple ID to the person using that computer, and then complete the following steps:

1. On the Advanced menu, choose **Turn On Home Sharing**. The Home Sharing icon appears in the Source pane, and you see the Home Sharing screen in the Content pane.

2. Enter the iTunes Store account and password associated with the content in the Library that you want make available for import.

3. Click **Create Home Share**. You see the confirmation screen.

4. Click **Done**. The Library associated with the source you selected appears in the Source pane; its icon is a house to indicate it is a Home Share source, as shown in Figure 12.3.

FIGURE 12.3   The Brad Miser's Library source is a Home Share source (note the House icon), and its content can be imported into this Library.

5. Select the shared source in the Source pane.

6. Click the **Settings** button. The Home Sharing Settings dialog appears. Use this to select new downloads (purchases) from the iTunes Store in the shared source to import automatically.

7. Check the check box for each type of content you want to be imported automatically, as shown in Figure 12.4.

FIGURE 12.4   Use this dialog to automatically import new content from the shared Library.

8. Click **OK**.

9. Repeat steps 1 through 8 on up to four other computers. Each of those computers can import content from the iTunes Library with which the iTunes Store account is associated.

Once a Home Sharing source is available, use it in the following ways:

▶ Expand or collapse the shared Library or any of its playlists or folders by clicking its triangle in the Source pane. When you use Home Sharing, you see everything included in the shared Library, including all its categories in the Library and all its playlists.

▶ To limit what you see to only those items not already in the current Library, choose **Items not in my library** from the Show menu. This is useful because it makes it easier to know which content doesn't already exist on the computer you are using.

▶ To import content, select the content you want to add and click the **Import** button. The content is copied from the sharing source into the Library. If the Show menu is set to Items not in my library, each item disappears from view as it is imported. Once imported, you can use the content just as you can other content in your Library.

▶ If you enabled the automatic transfer of content using the Home Sharing Settings dialog box, when the shared source is available and new content has been added, content of the types you selected is imported automatically.

▶ To disable Home Sharing, choose **Advanced**, **Turn Off Home Sharing**. The Home Sharing sources disappear from the Source pane, but the imported content remains in the Library.

Summary

In this lesson you learned how to use the sharing capabilities of iTunes to take advantage of multiple libraries on the same network. In the next lesson, you learn how to take your iTunes experience a little further with some advanced techniques.

LESSON 13

Burning CDs and DVDs

In this lesson, you learn how to use iTunes to move content from your iTunes Library onto CDs and DVDs. You also learn how to use iTunes to print jewel case inserts and album and song lists.

Preparing to Burn

Before you starting burning discs, you need to do a little prep work. This includes ensuring the disc drive you use to burn is ready to go and preparing content to burn onto discs.

Checking Your Disc Drive

To burn CDs or DVDs, your computer must have a drive capable of writing to CD or DVD. Fortunately, most computers include a CD-RW (CD-Rewritable) drive you can use to burn CDs. Most modern computers also include a DVD-R, DVD-RW, DVD+R, or DVD+RW drive you can use to create DVDs. The type of burning you do with iTunes is pretty basic, so unless the drive you use is very old, it is likely to support the formats iTunes can use to burn discs.

To determine whether your computer is ready to burn, select a playlist in the Source pane. Choose **File**, **Burn Playlist to Disc**. The Burn Settings dialog box appears, as shown in Figure 13.1 (Windows) and Figure 13.2 (Mac). At the top of this dialog box, you see the disc burners that iTunes has found. If iTunes can find one or more drives capable of burning CDs or DVDs, they are shown here. (If there is more than one drive available, use the drop-down list to select the drive to use.). If iTunes does recognize a drive, you are good to go and can proceed to the next section.

FIGURE 13.1　This Windows computer has a CD/DVD disc burner that is ready to burn.

FIGURE 13.2　This MacBook Pro includes a SuperDrive that can be used to burn CDs or DVDs.

If a drive is not shown in the dialog box, there are two possible reasons. One is that a capable drive is installed but is not functioning correctly, so it's not recognized by iTunes. The other is that your computer doesn't have a capable drive.

If your computer does have a drive capable of writing to a disc but it is not recognized by iTunes, it is likely that your drive is not working. In this case, use troubleshooting techniques to repair and configure the drive to get it working again. Troubleshooting can be complicated, and is beyond

the scope of this book. If you don't know how to do this or you don't
know someone who does, consult one of the many books available on this
topic to help you get the drive working properly.

> NOTE: **Drive Problems**
>
> In many cases, a drive that doesn't work properly can be fixed by
> updating the driver software for that drive. You might need to down-
> load and install the proper driver from your drive's manufacturer;
> some drivers are updated automatically when you run Windows
> Update. If you use a Mac that included a drive when you purchased
> it, the drivers are updated when you use the Software Update appli-
> cation.

Selecting and installing a CD-RW or DVD-RW drive in your computer is
beyond the scope of this book. If your computer doesn't have at least a
CD-RW drive, it is likely a fairly old machine, because these drives have
been standard on most computers for quite a while. Most current machines
include drive that can burn DVDs, too. If you don't want to purchase a
new computer that includes a writable drive, you can purchase an external
or internal CD-RW or DVD-RW drive and install it with your computer
fairly easily.

Understanding Disc Formats to Burn

You can burn several types of disc formats with iTunes, and each of these
formats is useful for specific purposes. With iTunes, you can burn the following types of discs:

- ▶ **Audio CD.** When you burn a CD in this format, you can play it
  in any CD player, such as the one in your car, a boombox, or a
  home theater. And that is the primary benefit of this format: CD
  players are ubiquitous, so you can play audio CDs just about
  anywhere.

- ▶ **MP3 CD.** You can place your tunes on a CD in the MP3 format
  and then play those discs using any player that can handle MP3

music. Many newer CD players for cars and home theater systems can play MP3 CDs, so this is a good thing. The benefit of using the MP3 format is just what you might think it is: You can put about three times as much music on a single disc as you can with a disc that uses the Audio CD format.

▶ **Data CD or DVD.** This format is the same that's used to store music files on your computer's hard drive. In fact, when you choose this format, you simply replicate songs as they are stored on your computer onto a disc. The primary purpose of this format is to back up your music to protect it from loss should something go horribly wrong with your computer. You can also copy songs to a disc to move them from one computer to another.

Preparing Playlists to Burn

The first phase in the process is to choose the content you want to place onto a disc; you do this by creating a playlist or by using an existing playlist. In Lesson 8, "Creating and Using Playlists," you learn everything you need to know about creating and using playlists, so that information doesn't need to be repeated here.

One thing you need to keep in mind as you create a playlist for CD or DVD is the size of the playlist. Obviously, you can't put more music on a CD or DVD than there is room to store files on the disc. How large a playlist can be for successful transfer to a disc depends on the format you are using. If you are burning an audio CD, you can get about 70 minutes of music on the disc. If you are creating an MP3 disc, you can store about 210 minutes on a disc. If you are creating a data CD, you can store about 750MB of data per disc. On a data DVD disc, you can store at least 4.7GB of files (twice as much if you use a dual-layer drive and disc).

When you are creating an audio CD, use the playing time to judge the size of the playlist; keep it to 70 minutes plus or minus a couple minutes. For the other formats, use file size. (For example, a CD can typically hold 750MB of data.)

Select the playlist you want to burn, and use the Source Information area
to check the playlist to make sure it will fit on the type of disc you are
going to create as shown in Figure 13.3.

Selected playlist

Source information

FIGURE 13.3   This playlist contains 1.1 hours of music, which will be just
right for a CD in the Audio CD format.

TIP: **No Rounding Please**

If you click once on the time displayed in the Source Information
area, you see the exact time to the second instead of the rounded-
off time. Click again to return to the rounded-off time.

If you choose to burn a playlist that contains more music than will fit on
the type of disc you are trying to burn, iTunes warns you about the situation. Then, you can choose to cancel the burn or choose to have iTunes
burn the playlist across multiple discs.

By default, the name of the playlist becomes the name of the CD or DVD.
If you don't want to use the current playlist name, just change it to whatever you want the disc to be called. To do this, click the playlist name

once and pause. It is highlighted to show you can change it. Type the new name and press Enter (Windows) or Return (Mac).

> NOTE: **How Much Music Can I Fit on a Disc?**
>
> The exact amount of music you can fit on a disc depends on your drive and the discs you use. The best way to figure out a maximum limit is to experiment until you find the upper limit for your system and the discs you use. Fortunately, iTunes helps you by telling you when you have selected more than will fit on a disc.

When you burn a disc in the Audio CD or Data CD or DVD formats, you don't have to worry about the format that the content of the playlist is in, and you are ready to move to the next session to burn the disc.

If you are going to burn a disc in the MP3 CD format, you must make sure all the music in the playlist you want to put on disc is in the MP3 format before you can burn the MP3 CD disc.

To see the format music is currently in, look for the Kind tag in a list when you are viewing the contents of the playlist you are going to burn, as shown in Figure 13.4. (You learned how to configure lists to show specific tags in Lesson 4, "Listening to Music.")

You are likely to encounter several different types of formats when attempting to burn an MP3 CD. Table 13.1 shows the three most common formats and how you can prepare content in that format for an MP3 CD.

TABLE 13.1   Suitability of Common Music File Formats for MP3 CD

Kind	Likely Source	Suitability for MP3 CD	Preparation
AAC audio file	iTunes Store, audio CD import	Fair	Convert to MP3 format
Protected AAC audio file	iTunes Store	Poor	Export to audio CD, import, convert to MP3 format
MPEG audio file	Amazon.com, audio CD import	Excellent	None

FIGURE 13.4 Use the Kind tag to identify the format of the songs you want to place on an MP3 CD.

You can use iTunes to directly convert music in the AAC audio file format into the MP3 format, as you learn in Lesson 14, "Going Further with iTunes." If you have protected AAC music (files with DRM applied), the process is more difficult because you can't directly convert this content into the MP3 format. You first have to burn the content onto an audio CD, then import that CD back into your Library, and finally convert it into MP3.

You can also store music in a number of other formats, such as Apple Lossless. In most cases, however, you can convert these other types into MP3 as you can the AAC audio file format.

CAUTION: **Converting Formats**

Every time you convert content in iTunes, a copy is made. This is good because the original file is kept intact. However, it is also bad because you end up with multiple copies of the same content in your Library, which can clutter it up and make working with music more difficult. You should rename converted content to indicate which is the converted file and which is the original so that they are easy to distinguish. If you need the converted content only once, you can delete it when you finish with it.

Burning Discs

After you've prepared a playlist to burn onto disc, the hard work is done. To burn the disc, just follow these steps:

1. Select the playlist you want to burn to disc, as shown in Figure 13.5.

FIGURE 13.5   Select the playlist you want to burn onto a CD in the Source pane.

2. Choose **File**, **Burn Playlist to CD**. The Burn Settings dialog box appears, as shown in Figure 13.6.

3. To burn a CD for use in standard CD players, click the **Audio CD** radio button and move to the next step; to burn a disc in the MP3 format, click the **MP3 CD** radio button and skip to step 7. To burn a data disc, click the **Data CD or DVD** radio button and skip to step 7.

4. Configure the **Gap Between Songs** setting. Your options are None, which causes one song to begin immediately after the previous one ends; 1 second, which places 1 second of silence between tracks; 2 seconds, which places 2 seconds of silence between songs; and so on, up to 5 seconds.

FIGURE 13.6 Use this dialog to configure and burn a disc.

5. If you want iTunes to set the relative volume levels of the songs on the disc to be the same, check the **Use Sound Check** check box.

> TIP: **Live Music**
> If you are putting live music on a disc, be sure you select **None** as the Gap Between Songs setting. Otherwise, the roar of the crowd will be interrupted by the silent gaps, which causes the live feeling to be lost.

6. To include additional information that some CD players can display, check the **Include CD Text** check box. This information includes title, artist, and so on. Some players will display all or just some of this text, whereas others may not be able to display any of it. There's not much reason to avoid including this; so in most cases, you should check this check box.

7. Click **Burn**. You're prompted to insert a blank disc; if your computer has a tray, it opens.

NOTE: **No Data DVD?**

If your system doesn't include a drive capable of burning DVDs, the third option is just data CD. If your system does include a DVD burner, this option is data CD or DVD.

8. Insert the appropriate disc into the drive. If you selected the Audio CD or MP3 CD format, use a CD. If you selected the Data format, use a CD or DVD. iTunes checks the disc you inserted. If everything checks out, the burn process starts, and you can monitor the process in the Information area, as shown in Figure 13.7.

FIGURE 13.7   The Information area displays progress information about the burn process.

If the playlist doesn't fit onto a single disc, iTunes fills the first disc with all the content that fits on the disc in whole (no partial songs), ejects it, and prompts you to insert another one. Do so, and the process continues.

If the disc can't be burned for some reason, iTunes displays an error message. You have to correct the situation before you can complete the burn.

When the process is complete, iTunes plays a tone to let you know. The disc you just burned appears on the Source list, as shown in Figure 13.8.

9. You can play the CD if you want to test it; click the **Eject** button when you're done. The disc is ejected and you can use the disc you created in any player or drive that is compatible with its format.

FIGURE 13.8   When the burn is done, you see the disc in the iTunes Source pane.

Printing Jewel Case Inserts and Lists

If create your own CDs and DVDs, you probably want to make labels for them to keep them organized and make them look nice. The good news is that iTunes can do some of this for you. You can use iTunes to print inserts for jewel cases (which are the plastic cases designed to store CDs, such as those you get when you buy a CD from a music store) you use to store discs, and you can also print lists to help you keep your discs organized.

NOTE: **iTunes Doesn't Do Labels**

Unfortunately, iTunes can't help you print disc labels that you apply directly to the discs you burn. If you want to label your discs, you need to use a different application. If labels are important to you, consider investing in a dedicated disc label creator application. If you use a Windows computer, many labeling applications are available, such as AudioLabel CD Labeler. If you use a Mac or a Windows computer, Discus enables you to create just about any disc label you can imagine.

Printing Jewel Case Inserts

iTunes can print jewel case inserts that you can use to label the cases in which you store the discs you burn.

For best results, associate artwork with the songs you put on a disc. When you create and print a jewel case insert, the artwork associated with the songs on the disc will become part of the insert. Fortunately, in many cases, iTunes handles this for you automatically. As you learn in Lesson 7, "Tagging iTunes Content," you can manually associate artwork with your content too.

To create a jewel case insert, follow these steps:

1. Select the playlist for which you want to create a jewel case insert; obviously, this should be the same one you used to burn the associated disc.

2. Select **File, Print**. You see the Print "*playlistname*" dialog box, where *playlistname* is the name of the playlist you selected, as you see in Figure 13.9.

FIGURE 13.9   Use this dialog box to configure and print a jewel case insert.

3. Click the **CD jewel case insert** radio button.

4. Use the **Theme** pop-up menu to select the type of insert you want to print. Some of the more useful options are explained in the following list:

▶ **Text only.** Prints a listing of the songs on the disc on the back of the insert over a colored background.

▶ **Mosaic.** Prints a collage of the artwork associated with songs in the playlist on the front and a list of the songs on the back. This is a color insert. If you choose the Mosaic theme and the songs included in the playlist have only a single piece of artwork (for instance, if they are all from the same album), that image fills the front of the insert.

▶ **White Mosaic.** This is similar to Mosaic, except it prints on a white background.

▶ **Single cover.** Places a single graphic on the front; the graphic of the selected song is used. It also includes a list of songs on the back.

▶ **Large playlist.** It doesn't include any artwork, but it does place the list of songs on the front and back of the insert. As you can tell by its name, it is intended for large playlists that have too many songs to be listed on the back of the other insert types.

▶ **Black & White versions.** These exist for each of these types in case you don't use a color printer or you just like the look of black-and-white inserts.

5. Click **Page Setup**. You see the Page Setup dialog box.

6. Configure the page setup to match the paper you are using for the insert. If you are using paper designed specifically for this purpose, you might have to experiment a bit to know which selection best matches the insert paper you are printing on. Unfortunately, iTunes doesn't support specific CD jewel case insert paper by brand and insert number (as a dedicated disc label application does).

7. When you have configured the page setup, click **OK**. You move back to the Print dialog box.

8. Click **OK** (Windows) or **Print** (Mac).

9. Use the resulting Print dialog box to configure and complete the print job.

10. Cut or tear out the insert and place it in the jewel case.

Printing Song and Album Lists

iTunes can print lists of songs and albums in any source in your Library. These can prove useful as catalogs of your music, so you know what you have burned onto a disc or have stored a specific sources in iTunes. Here's how to print a list:

1. Select the source for which you want to print a list.

2. Select **File**, **Print**. You see the Print "*playlistname*" dialog box, where *playlistname* is the name of the playlist you selected.

3. Click the **Song listing** radio button to print a list of songs in the selected source or the **Album listing** radio button to print a list of songs grouped by their albums.

4. If you select the Song listing option, select the theme for the list from the Theme drop-down list, as shown in Figure 13.10. The options are as follows:

   ▶ **Songs.** Prints the song name, length, artist, and album.

   ▶ **User ratings.** Adds your rating to the data in the Songs option.

   ▶ **Dates played.** This includes all the information in the Songs option plus the play count and date.

   ▶ **Custom.** Prints the data shown in the current view of the selected source. You can change the data included in the list by changing the View options for the source. (If you don't remember how to do this, refer to Lesson 4.)

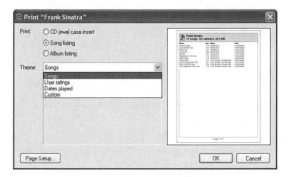

FIGURE 13.10 Song lists provide detail about the songs included in the selected source.

5. If you select the Album listing option, select the theme for the list from the Theme drop-down list from the following options:

   ▶ **Songs by album.** Organizes the listing by grouping songs into the albums from which they come and displays song details for each, including album name, artist, song title, and length.

   ▶ **List of albums.** Prints the albums included in the source with no song detail.

6. Click **OK** (Windows) or **Print** (Mac). The list prints on the printer you have selected.

Summary

In this lesson, you learned how to burn content from your iTunes Library onto CDs and DVDs. You also learned how to print jewel case inserts and lists. In the next lesson, you expand your iTunes education by tackling some advanced topics.

LESSON 14

Going Further with iTunes

In this lesson, you gain some additional skills to enable you to get even more out of iTunes and to protect your investment in it. The tasks include using Ping, backing up your iTunes content, converting media types, and more.

Working with Ping

When it comes to Ping, if you think iTunes meets Facebook, you have the gist of it. Ping enables you to both view information about events and items of interest to people you follow (such as bands or friends) and to keep people informed about music of interest to you by allowing people to follow you. You can access Ping in the iTunes Store, within the Ping pane in the iTunes window, and for specific songs in the Content pane.

Setting Up Ping

To get started, enable and configure Ping as follows:

1. Select **Ping** in the Store section on the Source list.

2. Click **Turn On Ping**.

3. Enter your Apple ID (if necessary), enter your password, and then click **OK**. You move to the Create My Profile page.

4. Complete your profile by creating a nickname, uploading a photo, and entering other information you want to include.

5. Click **Continue**.

6. On the second page of the Create My Profile form, configure how you want music displayed on your profile, such as **Automatically display all music I like, rate, review, or purchase**.

7. Click **Continue**.

8. Configure how you want to allow people to follow by clicking **Allow people to follow me** or **Don't allow people to follow me**.

9. If you allow people to follow you, check **Require my approval** if you want to be able to grant permission for people to follow you. If you leave this unchecked, anyone who wants to follow you, can.

10. Click **Done**. Ping is now set up within iTunes, and you see the Welcome to Ping screen.

Following Artists or Other People

When you follow a group, solo artist, or other iTunes Store user, you see information about what those people are doing. For example, you see information about a band's upcoming concerts, comments from members, songs people have rated or purchased, and so on. To follow artists or other Ping users, follow these steps steps:

1. Open the Ping menu on the iTunes Store menu bar and choose **People**. Then move to your People page. This page has two tabs: People I Follow and People Who Follow Me.

2. In the FIND PEOPLE box, enter the name of the artist or person you want to follow as shown in Figure 14.1 and press Enter (Windows) or Return (Mac). The artists and other people that can be followed and match your search are shown.

3. Click the **Follow** button for the artist or person you want to follow, as shown in Figure 14.2. If the artist or person doesn't require authorization for you to become a follower, you start following the artist or person immediately. If permission is required, the artist or person has to respond positively to a confirmation email before you can follow them. The status of that person will show Request sent until your request has been approved.

FIGURE 14.1   Use the Find People tool to search for artists or other Ping users you might want to follow.

FIGURE 14.2   Click the Follow button to start following artists or other Ping users.

NOTE: **No Following for You!**

If the person to whom you sent a follow request ignores your request, you won't receive a notification saying so. The request just stays with the status Request sent.

> TIP: **Browsing for Artists**
>
> To browse for artists to follow, click **See All** in the WE RECOM-MEND YOU FOLLOW section.

4. Click the **Previous Page** link. You move back to People page and can add more artists and people to follow.

> NOTE: **Follow Me If You Care To**
>
> If you'd like to see what I'm into from the musical perspective, feel free to follow by searching for Brad Miser, who lives in Brownsburg.

Inviting People to Follow You

To invite someone to follow you, complete the following steps:

1. Open the Ping menu on the iTunes Store menu bar and choose **People**.

2. Click the **Email** link in the FIND PEOPLE section.

3. Fill out the Invitation form and click **Invite** (see Figure 14.3). An email is sent to the person with the message you created. That person can then move to Ping and start following you.

FIGURE 14.3 Inviting others to follow you is easy; just complete this form and click **Invite**.

Using Ping

After Ping is set up, here are just some of the ways you can use it:

► Click the **Ping** option on the iTunes Store menu bar to move to your Ping home page. Here, you see activity related to the artists and people you follow. This can be announcements, new releases of music, people rating or purchasing music, and so on. You can also comment on the events, view all comments, and buy music or concert tickets.

► Move to your People page by choosing **People** on the Ping menu or clicking **People** on your Ping home page. Click the **People I Follow** tab to view the artists and people you are following. If you click a name, you move to the artist's or person's profile page, where you can see various information about the person (band), recent activity, and so on (depending on the security settings of their account). Click the **People Who Follow Me** tab to see what is happening with people who are following you. In either case, you can explore activity by browsing the screen or clicking links, such as **My Reviews** to read reviews the person has posted.

► To change your profile at any time, click the **My Profile** link in the Ping section on your Ping home page, click the **Edit Profile** link, and use the resulting screens to make and save your changes.

► To use Ping within the iTunes window, open the iTunes sidebar by choosing **View**, **Show iTunes Sidebar** or by clicking the **Show iTunes Sidebar** button in the lower-right corner of the window. The sidebar opens, and you see information related to what is selected in the Content pane in the upper section of the sidebar and the My Recent Activity in the lower part, as shown in Figure 14.4. For example, if you select music by an artist you are following, see you information about that artist. In the My Recent Activity section, you see a partial view of your Ping home page. Click **See All** to move to your Ping home page. At the bottom of the pane, you see the Genius Recommendations section that shows music that might of interest to you.

FIGURE 14.4   Use the iTunes sidebar to view information about artists you are listening to and to see what is happening on your Ping home page.

▶ When you select a song, the Ping menu appears in the Name column. Open the Ping menu and choose **Like** to show everyone you like the song, **Post** to post a comment about the song and share it with people who follow you, or **Show Artist Profile** to move to the artist's Ping page.

Backing Up iTunes Content

This might be the most important section in this book, especially if you download a significant amount of content from the iTunes Store. That's because you can download music and video content only once. If something happens to your computer (or even the content you download) and you can't use it any more, you cannot download it again without paying for it again. And, even if you have imported content from CDs, it takes time to do that, and who wants to redo something you have already done?

You need to regularly and often back up your iTunes content so you can recover it should something happen. There are two basic backup approaches for your iTunes content:

▶ **Use a backup system.** This is the best option because it protects all the information stored on your computer, including your iTunes content.

▶ **Use the iTunes backup feature.** This also protects your iTunes content, but won't help you recover anything else. It is also useful as a permanent way to store your content as a second back up to your back-up system.

CAUTION: **Not Backing Up Can Cost You Lots of Money**

Backing up is especially critical for music, audiobooks, and video you purchase from the iTunes Store. If something happens to that content, you can't download it again without paying for it again. If you lose files you have purchased and don't have a backup, they are gone forever (unless you pay for them again, that is).

Backing Up with a Backup System

You have a lot more than iTunes content on your computer, and you should keep all your information, documents, applications, and so on backed up. There are many ways to set up a backup system, and the details of doing so are beyond the scope of this lesson.

You can use a backup application with a local hard drive, online storage, or DVDs to back up content locally. There are also online backup services that protect your computer's content by copying it to remote servers.

When you use a backup system, make sure your iTunes content is included in the files to be backed up. Should anything happen to that content on your computer, you can use your backup system to restore it.

Backing Up with iTunes

iTunes includes a backup function that you can use to burn your iTunes Library onto CDs or DVDs. If your Library includes video content, you want to be able to use DVDs because video content requires a lot of storage space. To back up with iTunes, complete the following steps:

1. Choose **File**, **Library**, **Back Up to Disc**. You see the iTunes Backup dialog box, as shown in Figure 14.5.

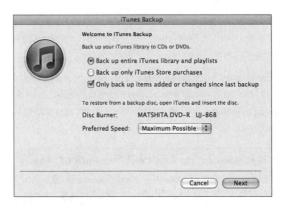

FIGURE 14.5   You should back up your iTunes content to DVD or CD periodically, even if you use a backup system.

2. Click **Back up entire iTunes library and playlists** if you want to be able restore all your iTunes content or click **Back up only iTunes Store purchases** if you want to back up only content you've purchased from the iTunes Store. If you have a large Library, choosing the first option can require lots of discs and time, but it's likely worth it if you think about the time it took for you to build your Library. I recommend that you choose the first option all the time. You can use the incremental backup feature to limit the number of discs you use.

3. To enable iTunes to perform incremental backups, check the **Only back up items added or changed since last backup** check box. I recommend that you check this box because after the first time iTunes backs up your Library, it only backs up changed items from then on, which saves you discs and time during subsequent backups.

4. Click **Next**. You're prompted to insert at blank disc.

5. Insert a blank DVD or CD. (Use DVDs if your computer has a DVD burner because it will require a lot fewer discs.) iTunes determines what needs to be backed up.

6. If some content can't be back up, you see a warning dialog showing how many files can't be backed up. You can expand this to

see the specific tracks that can't be backed up and why they can't be. You can review this information to determine if or how to fix the problem. Click **OK** to close the warning dialog box and continue the backup process.

7. If the backup requires more than one disc, you see a prompt explaining this is the case and showing you how many discs you need to complete the backup. Click **Continue** to continue. iTunes starts the backup process and begins burning content to the disc you inserted. As it fills up discs, the full discs are ejected, and you're prompted to insert a new blank disc.

8. Remove and label each disc as iTunes ejects it and insert a new blank disc until the process is complete. You should label each disc so that you know it's an iTunes backup disc. You also need to number the disc and include the date on which you burned it. The number is important when you restore content because it helps you identify which disc to insert.

The first time you back up, this process takes a long time and consumes many discs. Fortunately, because iTunes can back up incrementally, subsequent backups require much less time and fewer discs. You continue to use iTunes and other applications while the backup process happens.

NOTE: **Not Really a Back Up, But....**

In Lesson 12, "Sharing iTunes Content on a Local Network," you learned how to import content from one Library into another on the same network. After you import content, it exists in two places (or more if you import it to multiple computers). This can serve as a back up for you because you could re-import content back into a library should something happen to it. However, unless you are sure you have imported all your content into at least one other Library, you shouldn't rely on this as your only backup.

Configuring Where iTunes Content is Stored

When iTunes is installed on a computer, the iTunes Media folder is created. As you can guess from its name, this is where iTunes stores all the content in your Library. The default location of this folder depends on the kind of computer you are using. On Windows computers, the folder is stored in a folder called iTunes, located within your My Music folder (which, in turn, is located in various other folders depending on the version of Windows you are using). On Macs, this folder is also called iTunes, but it is located in the Music folder within your Home folder.

To see the current location of the iTunes Music folder on your computer, open the iTunes Preferences dialog box and click the **Advanced** tab. At the top of this dialog box, you see the iTunes Media folder location box. Within this box, you see the path to your iTunes Media folder.

NOTE: **iTunes Music Folder?**

If iTunes has been installed on your computer for some time, you might see the iTunes Music folder rather than the iTunes Media folder. That's because originally iTunes could only manage music, and so that name made sense. As it became able to handle other kinds of media, the name was changed to iTunes Media. However, if iTunes was installed prior to that change, the original name of the folder remains.

In most cases, the default location of your iTunes Media folder is fine, and you don't have to do anything about it. However, in some cases, you want to change the location of this folder. For example, suppose you have several hard drives in your computer, and the one on which the folder is currently stored doesn't have a lot of room. You might want to change the location of your iTunes Media folder so that it is on a drive with more room.

To change the location of this folder, do the following:

1. Click the **Advanced** tab of the iTunes Preferences dialog box.

2. Click the **Change** button. On a Windows PC, you see the Browse for Folder dialog box. On a Mac, you see the Change Media Folder Location dialog box.

3. Use the dialog box to move to and select the location in which you want your iTunes Media folder to be stored.

4. Click **OK** (Windows) or **Choose** (Mac). You return to the Advanced pane, and the folder you selected is shown in the iTunes Media folder location area.

5. Click **OK** to close the iTunes Preferences dialog box.

Changing the location of the iTunes Media folder won't hurt you. When you select a new folder, iTunes remembers the location of any previous content you have added to your Library and updates its database so that content is part of your Library.

The location of the folder in which your content is stored is likely the most important part of the organization preferences. However, you should understand a few more things to keep your content nicely organized and available:

▶ **Keep iTunes Media folder organized check box.** This preference, located on the Advanced pane, causes iTunes to organize content files by album and artist folders and names files based on the disc number, track number, and the song title. This is a pretty logical way to organize your files, so I recommend that you leave this option active by making sure this check box is checked.

▶ **Copy files to iTunes Media folder when adding to library.** This preference, also on the Advanced pane, causes iTunes to make a copy of files that already exist on your computer (such as MP3 files you have downloaded from the Internet) and places those copies in your iTunes Media folder, just like files you download from the iTunes Store. If this preference is inactive, iTunes uses a pointer to song files you are adding instead of making a copy of the files; it doesn't actually place the files in your iTunes Media folder. The benefit of this option is that all your content files are in one folder (the iTunes Media folder). The downside is that you may end up with multiple copies of the same content files, which wastes disk space.

▶ **File, Library, Organize Library.** Use this command on the File menu to open the Organize Library dialog box. This has two options: Consolidate files and Upgrade to iTunes Media organization. Consolidate Files places copies of all media files in the iTunes Media folder. This creates a copy of content files not already there and places them in that folder. This is really useful if you change the location of your iTunes Media folder (for instance, putting it on a different disk) and want to have all your content stored there. It takes a lot of disk space, however, because it makes copies of all content files not already stored in the new folder. Upgrade to iTunes Media organization causes iTunes to change the older iTunes Music folder into the current iTunes Media folder and reorganize its contents accordingly. You can, and only need to, use this command once.

Using iTunes to Convert Media Types

You might sometimes want to convert media into different types. For example, you might want to change a song that is current in the AAC format into the MP3 format so that you can put it on an MP3 disc. Or, you might want to reformat a video for an iPhone. iTunes has some basic conversion tools built in.

Converting Audio into Different Formats

To convert audio files, use a two-step process. The first step is to choose the format into which you want to convert the audio content. The second step is to convert the audio.

To choose the format into which you are converting audio, complete the following steps:

1. Click the **General** tab of the iTunes Preferences dialog box.

2. Click **Import Settings**.

3. On the Import Using menu, choose the format into which you want to convert the audio content (**MP3 Encoder**, for example).

4. Click **OK** to close the Import Settings dialog box.

5. Click **OK** to close the iTunes Preferences dialog box.

To convert audio content into the format you selected in the previous steps, select the songs you want to convert and choose **Advanced**, **Create *Format* Version**, where *Format* is the option you selected on the Import Using menu. Copies of the selected songs in the format you indicated are made.

> NOTE: **Mind Your Disk Space**
> When you convert content, a copy is created. This means you have two versions of the same content (albeit in different formats) in your Library. This uses more disk space, which isn't always a good thing. If you don't need both versions, delete the copies you don't need to free up the disk space on which they were stored.

Converting Video into Different Formats

iTunes has a little-known, but very handy, tool you can use to convert video content into versions that are compatible with iPods/iPhones or iPads/Apple TV.

Using this converter is simple. Select the video file you want to convert and choose **Advanced**, **Create iPod or iPhone Version** or **Advanced**, **Create iPad or Apple TV Version**. A copy of the content in the selected format is made, although it can take a long time.

Working with Authorization

Some of the content you purchase from the iTunes Store is protected with digital rights management (DRM). (In Lesson 2, "Working with the iTunes Store," you learned about DRM in detail.) To play DRM-protected content on a computer, it must be authorized for the account under which that content was purchased.

Authorizing a Computer

You can authorize a computer by choosing **Store**, **Authorize This Computer**. In the resulting dialog box, enter the **account information** for which you want to authorize it and click **Authorize**. When the process is complete, you see a message telling you how many computers are authorized under the account; click **OK** to close the dialog box. You can then play content purchased under the account.

If you attempt to authorize more than five computers under the same user account, a warning prompt explains that you can have only five computers authorized at the same time. You must deauthorize one of the computers to be able to authorize another one.

> NOTE: **Play to Authorize**
> If you play content for which a computer isn't authorized, you are prompted to authorize the computer, which does the same thing as using the command on the Store menu.

Deauthorizing a Computer

To deauthorize a computer, select **Store, Deauthorize This Computer**. In the resulting dialog box, enter the **account information** for which you want to deauthorize the computer and click **Deauthorize**. When the process is complete, you see a dialog box telling you so. Click **OK**. The computer no longer counts against the five-computer limit for the user account. (You aren't able to play content purchased under that iTunes Store account on that computer, either.)

> NOTE: **Deauthorize All**
> If five computers are authorized for your account and you want to "start over," you can deauthorize all the computers simultaneously by clicking **Store** and then clicking your account name. In the resulting dialog box, enter your password and click **View Account**. Click **Deauthorize All**.

Summary

In this lesson, you learned how to take your iTunes skills to the next level and use some of iTunes advanced features. In the next lesson, you learn how to resolve problems you might experience with iTunes.

LESSON 15

Solving Problems

In this lesson, you learn how to solve problems you might encounter when using iTunes.

Solving iTunes Problems

This is a short chapter for good reason. iTunes is a stable and reliable application, and it's likely you won't have to spend much time troubleshooting and solving problems. Still, you might encounter an issue from time to time, so it's good to know what to do. This section contains a general approach that solves most problems you may encounter, along with a couple of specific issues and their solutions. Later in this lesson, you learn how to get help if these solutions don't work.

Solving General Problems

Fortunately, most problems can be solved with the following general solutions:

▶ **Restart iTunes.** It's amazing how many issues you can solve by just restarting iTunes. This should be one of the first things you try when you encounter a problem. Just quit iTunes and launch it again. If the problem is gone, you're done. If not, keep going.

▶ **Restart your computer.** This is the other easy solution to many problems you may experience. Simply restart your computer, and then open iTunes. In many cases, the problem you were having is "magically" cured.

▶ **Update iTunes.** Apple is pretty good about releasing bug fixes through updates to the iTunes application. When you are having problems, make sure you are using the current version of iTunes, and if not, update it. To update iTunes on a Windows PC, choose **Help**, **Check For Updates**. On a Mac, open the iTunes menu and choose **Check For Updates**. If a new version is available, you are prompted to download and install it. After you download and install the update, launch iTunes to check to whether the update resolved the problem.

TIP: **Automatic Updates**

You should configure iTunes to automatically check for updates. Open the General pane of the iTunes Preferences dialog box. Then check the **Check for new software updates automatically** check box. When iTunes finds an update, you're prompted to download and install it.

▶ **Reinstalling iTunes.** If none of the previous solutions work and you aren't experiencing one of the specific issues covered in the following sections, you can try reinstalling iTunes. This is more common solution on Windows PCs than it is on Macs, but you can try it on either platform when nothing else seems to work. Use the tools built in to Windows to remove iTunes; the specific tools available depend on the version of Windows you are using. On a Mac, drag the iTunes application icon from the Applications folder into the Trash, and then empty the Trash. After you remove iTunes, reinstall it using the steps you learn in Lesson 1, "Getting Started with iTunes."

NOTE: **What About iTunes Content?**

iTunes stores content, such as music and video, in a different location than where the application is stored. You can reinstall iTunes without disturbing your iTunes content. Of course, you should always have your iTunes content backed up (for instance, stored on DVD or an external hard drive) in case something happens to your computer. If a problem with your computer causes you to lose music or video you've purchased from the iTunes Store, you have to pay for it again to be able to download it and restore it to your Library. So, be sure you back up your iTunes content regularly. (You learned how to back up in Lesson 14, "Going Further with iTunes.")

Solving the Missing-Content Problem

One problem you might encounter occasionally has nothing to do with iTunes not working properly. This problem occurs when something happens to the files that contain content in your Library. The indication that you are having this problem is iTunes displaying an Exclamation Point icon next to any content whose files it can't find when you try to play that content (or try to do anything else with it, for that matter). Figure 15.1 shows an example.

FIGURE 15.1   When you see the Exclamation Point icon next to items in your Library, iTunes can't find the files in which the content is stored.

The most likely cause of this problem is that the files for the missing content have been moved or deleted outside of iTunes.

To fix this problem, you have to reconnect iTunes to the missing file. Here are the steps to follow:

1. Double-click an item for which the Exclamation Point icon is shown. A prompt tells you that the content's file can't be found and asks whether you want to locate it, as shown in Figure 15.2.

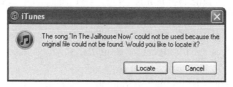

FIGURE 15.2   You see this prompt when iTunes can't find content you are trying to play.

2. Click **Locate**. You see the iTunes dialog box on a Windows PC or the Choose a File : iTunes dialog box on a Mac.

3. Move to the content's file, select it, and click **Open** (Windows) or **Choose** (Mac). You see a dialog asking whether you want iTunes to try to find other missing content based on the location of the missing content you found, as shown in Figure 15.3.

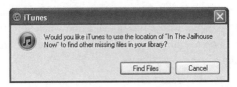

FIGURE 15.3   iTunes tries to restore other missing content based on the location in which you manually found missing content.

4. Click **Find Files**. iTunes searches the location for any other content missing. You see the results in a dialog box like that shown in Figure 15.4.

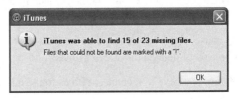

FIGURE 15.4   iTunes tells you how successful it was finding other missing content.

5. Click **OK**. This missing content iTunes was able to locate is restored and the problem is solved—for that content. You return to the iTunes window, and the content you selected originally begins to play. If iTunes wasn't able to find some of the missing content, you have to locate it using the previous steps.

Following are some additional notes about this issue:

▶ If you can't find content files on your computer, you have to restore that content from a backup. You learn how to do a restore later in this lesson. (You learned how to back up your iTunes content in Lesson 14.)

▶ If iTunes couldn't find the content because the files had been moved, you might want to cause iTunes to place that content back into the iTunes folder to keep your content files well organized. To do this, select **File, Organize Library**. In the resulting dialog box, check the **Consolidate files** and **Upgrade to iTunes Media organization** check boxes. Click **OK**. iTunes copies the missing files into the proper location (within your iTunes folder). It also reorganizes the files according to the proper subfolders. When you've confirmed all the content has been restored, you can delete the files from the original location.

Solving the "Missing iPod/iPhone/iPad/Apple TV" Problem

This problem means iTunes doesn't recognize that one of these devices is connected and that it isn't displayed in the Source pane. In this case, you can't use iTunes to sync its contents, restore it, or configure it. There can be several causes for this issue, but usually one of the following actions solves it:

▶ **Restart your computer.** In most cases, this restores the link between the device and iTunes the next time you connect the device to your computer.

▶ **Make sure the device isn't just out of power.** When an iPod, iPhone, or iPad runs completely out of power, it won't start up, and so can't be mounted in the Source pane. Leave the device connected to your computer for a few minutes. If it was just out of power, when the battery recharges a small amount, you see the charging screen on the device, and it becomes available in the Source pane.

▶ **Try a different USB port.** Not all USB ports are the same. Try to use a port that is part of the computer rather than one on an external device, even if you have to disconnect another device from that port temporarily. If the device becomes available in the Source pane, you know the issue is related to the port you were using.

▶ **Run Apple's web-based device assistant.** Move to http:// support.apple.com/kb/TS1495 (Windows) or http://support.apple. com/kb/TS1591?viewlocale=en_US (Mac). Click the link for the device you are troubleshooting and use the resulting assistant to troubleshoot the problem. If the assistant doesn't solve the issue, refer to the other information on these pages for more things to try.

Restoring iTunes Content

If something happens to your iTunes content, such as a hard disk problem, that causes you to lose that content, you need to restore it from a backup.

Of course, you have to have made and maintained backups for this to be useful. In Lesson 14, you learn about options for backing up your iTunes content. If there's only one thing you get out of this book (hopefully, you get a lot more than one thing), I hope it is the need to keep your iTunes content backed up. If not, you could lose lots of money because you can only download audio and video content that you paid for from the iTunes Store once. If you lose it and don't have a backup, it's gone forever and you have to pay for it again. When you lose content on audio CDs or DVDs that you imported, it takes a lot of time to reimport that content. Being able to restore content is the fastest and least expensive way to restore missing content.

As you learn in Lesson 14, there are two general ways to back up your content: using iTunes or using a back-up system outside of iTunes. How you restore your iTunes content depends on which method you use to back it up.

Restoring with iTunes

If you use iTunes back-up functionality, you can restore you content with the following steps:

1. Insert a **disc** containing content you backed up with iTunes.

2. Click **Restore** in the prompt.

3. Follow the onscreen instructions to restore the content. If it is stored on multiple discs, you're prompted to insert the next disc as the content on the current one is restored.

Restoring from a Backup System

If you use a back-up system, such as Time Machine on a Mac, use that system to restore your iTunes content. The steps to do this depend on the specific system you are using, but all systems have a restore option, which is the whole point of these systems.

Getting Help

When you run into a problem you can't solve yourself, there's lots of help available for you:

▶ **iTunes Help.** Choose **Help**, **iTunes Help** to access iTunes Help. You can search or browse the available help.

▶ **Apple's website.** Go to **www.apple.com/support/**. On this page, you can access all kinds of information about iTunes and other Apple products. You can browse and search for answers to problems. Many of the articles have detailed, step-by-step instructions to help you solve problems and link to more information.

▶ **Web searches.** One of the most useful ways to get help is to do a Web search for the specific problem you're having. Just open your favorite search tool, such as Google, and search for the problem. You are likely to find many resources to help you, including websites, forums, and such. If you encounter a problem, it's likely someone else has, too, and has probably put the solution on the Web.

▶ **Me.** You're welcome to send email to me for problems you're having with iTunes. My address is bradmiser@me.com. I'll do my best to help you as quickly as I can.

Summary

In this lesson, you learned how to solve iTunes problems.

Index

How can we make this index more useful? Email us at indexes@samspublishing.com

FREE Online Edition

Your purchase of **Sams Teach Yourself iTunes 10 in 10 Minutes** includes access to a free online edition for 45 days through the Safari Books Online subscription service. Nearly every Sams book is available online through Safari Books Online, along with more than 5,000 other technical books and videos from publishers such as Addison-Wesley Professional, Cisco Press, Exam Cram, IBM Press, O'Reilly, Prentice Hall, and Que.

SAFARI BOOKS ONLINE allows you to search for a specific answer, cut and paste code, download chapters, and stay current with emerging technologies.

Activate your FREE Online Edition at www.informit.com/safarifree

STEP 1: Enter the coupon code: VZGEHBI.

STEP 2: New Safari users, complete the brief registration form. Safari subscribers, just log in.

If you have difficulty registering on Safari or accessing the online edition, please e-mail customer-service@safaribooksonline.com